Board of Immigration Appeals Practice Manual

Table of Contents

Chapter 1 The Board of Immigration Appeals

1.1   Scope of the Board of Immigration Appeals Practice Manual

(a) Authority — The Board of Immigration Appeals has the authority to prescribe rules governing proceedings before it. 8 C.F.R. § 1003.1(d)(4).

(b) Purpose — This Practice Manual describes procedures, requirements, and recommendations for practice before the Board of Immigration Appeals (Board). This Practice Manual is provided for the information and convenience of the general public and for parties that appear before the Board.

(c) Disclaimer — This Practice Manual does not carry the weight of law or regulation. This manual is not intended, nor should it be construed in any way, as legal advice, nor does it extend or limit the jurisdiction of the Board as established by law and regulation.

(d) Revisions — The Board reserves the right to amend, suspend, or revoke the text of this Practice Manual at its discretion. Parties should consult the most recent version of the Practice Manual, which is posted on EOIR's website. To obtain updates of this manual, see Chapter 14.2 (Updates to the Board Practice Manual).

1.2   Function of the Board

(a) Role — The Board of Immigration Appeals (Board) is the highest administrative body for interpreting and applying immigration laws. The Board is responsible for applying the immigration and nationality laws uniformly throughout the United States. Accordingly, the Board has been given nationwide jurisdiction to review the orders of immigration judges and certain decisions made by the Department of Homeland Security (DHS), and to provide guidance to the immigration judges, DHS, and others, through published decisions. The Board is tasked with resolving the questions before it in a manner that is timely, impartial, and consistent with the Immigration and Nationality Act and regulations, and to provide clear and uniform guidance to immigrations judges, DHS, and the general public on the proper interpretation and administration of the Immigration and Nationality Act and its implementing regulations. 8 C.F.R. § 1003.1(d)(1).

The Board also has authority regarding the discipline of recognized organizations and practitioners appearing before the immigration courts, DHS, and the Board. See Chapter 11 (Discipline).

(b) Location within the Federal Government — The Board of Immigration Appeals is a component of the Executive Office for Immigration Review (EOIR) and, along with the Office of the Chief Immigration Judge (OCIJ) and the Office of the Chief Administrative Hearing Officer (OCAHO), operates under the supervision of the Director of the Executive Office for Immigration Review. See 8 C.F.R. § 1003.0(a). In turn, EOIR is a component of the Department of Justice and operates under the authority and supervision of the Attorney General. See Appendix B (Organizational Chart).

(c) Relationship to the Immigration Court — The Office of the Chief Immigration Judge (OCIJ) oversees the administration of the immigration courts nationwide and exercises administrative supervision over immigration judges. The immigration judges, as independent adjudicators, make determinations of removability, deportability, and excludability, and adjudicate applications for relief. The Board, in turn, reviews the decisions of the immigration judges. The decisions of the Board are binding on the immigration judges, unless modified or overruled by the Attorney General or a federal court. See Chapters 1.4(a) (Jurisdiction), 1.4(d) (Board Decisions). For detailed guidance on practice before the immigration courts, consult the Immigration Court Practice Manual.

(d) Relationship to the Department of Homeland Security (DHS) — The Department of Homeland Security was created in 2002 and assumed most of the responsibilities of the now abolished Immigration and Naturalization Service (INS). DHS is responsible for the enforcement of the immigration laws and the administration of immigration and naturalization benefits. In contrast, the Board and the immigration courts are responsible for the independent adjudication of cases under the immigration and nationality laws. Thus, DHS is entirely separate from the Department of Justice and is deemed a party when appearing before the Board or an immigration court. See Chapters 1.4(a) (Jurisdiction), 1.4(d) (Board Decisions), 1.4(f) (Department of Homeland Security).

(e) Relationship to the former Immigration and Naturalization Service (INS) — Prior to the creation of the Department of Homeland Security (DHS), the Immigration and Naturalization Service (INS) was the component of the Department of Justice responsible for the enforcement of the immigration laws and the administration of immigration benefits. The role of the INS has now been assumed by the DHS. See subsection (d), above.

(f) Relationship to other EOIR Offices —

(1) Office of the Chief Administrative Hearing Officer (OCAHO) — The Office of the Chief Administrative Hearing Officer (OCAHO) is an independent entity within EOIR. OCAHO is responsible for hearings involving employer sanctions, and document fraud under the Immigration and Nationality Act. The Board does not review decisions made by OCAHO. Additional information regarding OCAHO, is available on the EOIR website.

(2) Office of the General Counsel — The Office of the General Counsel (OGC) for EOIR provides legal advice to all of EOIR, including the Board. OGC is responsible for Freedom of Information Act (FOIA) requests for information from the Board. See Chapter 13 (Requesting Records), Appendix A (Directory). OGC is also responsible for receiving complaints about practitioners and recognized organizations and initiates disciplinary proceedings when appropriate. See Chapter 11 (Discipline). OGC is also responsible for administering EOIR's Fraud Program, which was created to protect the integrity of immigration proceedings by reducing immigration fraud and abuse. Individuals wishing to report immigration fraud or abuse, or other irregular activity, should contact the EOIR Fraud Program. For contact information, see Appendix A (Directory).

(3) Office of Policy —

(A) Communications and Legislative Affairs Division — The Communications and Legislative Affairs Division (CLAD) of EOIR's Office of Policy is responsible for public relations for EOIR. CLAD serves as the Board's liaison with the press. See Appendix A (Directory). CLAD houses EOIR's Law Library and Immigration Research Center (LLIRC). This law library is maintained for the staff of EOIR and is open to the public. See Chapter 1.5(b) (Library). The LLIRC also maintains a "Virtual Law Library" that is accessible at EOIR's website. The Virtual Law Library serves as a comprehensive repository of immigration-related law and information for use by practitioners and the general public. The site serves as a complement to the LLIRC located within the headquarters complex of EOIR.

(B) Office of Legal Access Programs — The Office of Legal Access Programs (OLAP) of EOIR's Office of Policy is responsible for improving access to representation for persons appearing before the immigration courts and the Board. The Assistant Director for Policy, through OLAP, administers the Recognition and Accreditation Program, including the recognition of organizations and the accreditation of their representatives wishing to appear before the immigration courts, the Board, and/or DHS. More information on OLAP is available on the EOIR website.

(C) Legal Education and Research Services Division — The Legal Education and Research Services (LERS) Division of EOIR's Office of Policy develops and coordinates headquarters and nationwide substantive legal training and professional development for new and experienced judges, attorneys, and others within EOIR who are directly involved in EOIR's adjudicative functions.

(g) Relationship to the Administrative Appeals Office (AAO) — The Administrative Appeals Office (AAO), previously referred to as the Administrative Appeals Unit (AAU), is a component of DHS. The AAO is responsible for adjudicating appeals from DHS denials of certain kinds of applications and petitions, including employment-based immigrant petitions and most nonimmigrant visa petitions. See 8 C.F.R. §§ 103.2, 103.3. The AAO is not a component of EOIR and should not be confused with EOIR or the Board. See Appendix B (Org Chart).

(h) Relationship to the Office of Immigration Litigation (OIL) — The Office of Immigration Litigation (OIL) conducts civil trial and appellate litigation in the federal courts and represents the United States in civil suits brought against the federal government regarding the movement of citizens and noncitizens across U.S. borders. OIL is a separate and distinct component of the Department of Justice, located within the Civil Division, and should not be confused with EOIR or the Board. See Appendix B (Org Chart).

1.3   Composition of the Board

(a) General — The Board consists of 23 Board Members, also known as Appellate Immigration Judges, including a Chairman and up to two Vice Chairmen. Under the direction of the Chairman, the Board uses a case management system to screen all cases and manage its caseload. 8 C.F.R. § 1003.1(e). Under this system, the Board adjudicates cases in one of three ways:

(1) Individual — The majority of cases at the Board are adjudicated by a single Board Member. In general, a single Board Member decides the case unless the case falls into one of seven categories that require a decision by a panel of three Board Members. These categories are:

- the need to settle inconsistencies among the rulings of different immigration judges

- the need to establish a precedent construing the meaning of laws, regulations, or procedures

- the need to review a decision by an immigration judge or DHS that is not in conformity with the law or with applicable precedents

- the need to resolve a case or controversy of major national import

- the need to review a clearly erroneous factual determination by an immigration judge

- the need to reverse the decision of an immigration judge or DHS in a final order, other than nondiscretionary dispositions, or

- the need to resolve a complex, novel, unusual, or recurring issue of law or fact.

(2) Panel — Cases not suitable for consideration by a single Board Member are adjudicated by a panel consisting of three Board Members. The panel of three Board Members renders decisions by majority vote. Cases are assigned to specific panels pursuant to the Chairman's administrative plan. The Chairman may change the composition of the sitting panels and may reassign Board Members from time to time.

(3) En banc — The Board may, by majority vote or by direction of the Chairman, assign a case or group of cases for full en banc consideration. 8 C.F.R. § 1003.1(a)(5). By regulation, en banc proceedings are not favored.

(b) Chairman and Vice Chairman — The Chairman, also known as the Chief Appellate Immigration Judge, directs, supervises, and establishes internal operating procedures and policies for the Board. The Chairman is assisted in the performance of their duties by one or two Vice Chairmen, also known as Deputy Chief Appellate Immigration Judges. The Chairman and Vice Chairmen are sitting Board Members.

(c) Board Members — Board Members, including the Chairman and the Vice Chairmen, adjudicate cases coming before the Board. 8 C.F.R. § 1003.1(a)(2)(i)(E).

Board Members may recuse themselves under any circumstances considered sufficient to require such action. A vacancy, absence, or unavailability of a Board Member does not impair the right of the remaining members to exercise all the powers of the Board. When circumstances so warrant, immigration judges, retired Board Members, retired immigration judges, Administrative Law Judges, and senior EOIR attorneys with at least ten years of experience in the field of immigration law may be designated as Temporary Board Members. 8 C.F.R. § 1003.1(a)(4). Parties appearing before the Board may not request specific Board Members or a specific panel to adjudicate their case. The Board also does not entertain inquiries regarding the identity of the panel or Board Members assigned to a pending case.

(d) Legal Staff — The Board employs a legal staff assigned to support designated panels, Board Members, and other Board functions. See generally 8 C.F.R. § 1003.1(a)(6).

(e) Clerk's Office — The Office of the Clerk is responsible for managing appellate records and information for the Board. The Clerk's Office is headed by the Chief Clerk of the Board. Cases in which a respondent is not detained are processed by two regional teams (East and West), depending on the location of the immigration court. Cases involving detained respondents are processed by the Priority Case Management team. The Docket team processes adjudicated cases and serves decisions on parties. Various other teams provide management and administrative support to all operations.

1.4   Jurisdiction and Authority

(a) Jurisdiction — The Board generally has the authority to review appeals from the following:

- decisions of immigration judges in removal, deportation, and exclusion proceedings (with some limitations on decisions involving voluntary departure), pursuant to 8 C.F.R. § 1003.1(b)(1), (2), (3)

- decisions of immigration judges pertaining to asylum, withholding of deportation, withholding of removal, Temporary Protected Status, the Convention Against Torture, and other forms of relief

- decisions of immigration judges on motions to reopen where the proceedings were conducted in absentia

- decisions of immigration judges in rescission of adjustment of status cases, as provided in 8 C.F.R. part 1246

- some decisions pertaining to bond, parole, or detention, as provided in 8 C.F.R part 1236, subpart A

- decisions of DHS on family-based immigrant petitions, the revocation of family-based immigrant petitions, and the revalidation of family-based immigrant petitions (except orphan petitions)

- decisions of DHS regarding waivers of inadmissibility for nonimmigrants under § 212(d)(3)(A)(ii) of the Immigration and Nationality Act

- decisions of DHS involving administrative fines and penalties under 8 C.F.R. part 1280

See 8 C.F.R. §§ 1003.1(b), 1292.3. The Board may review these matters either upon appeal by one of the parties or by certification. See 8 C.F.R. § 1003.1(b), (c). Regarding the Board's scope of review, see Chapter 1.4(c) (Scope of Review).

The Board also has the authority to discipline practitioners and recognized organizations for professional misconduct, as discussed in Chapter 11 (Discipline).

(b) No Jurisdiction — Although the Board exercises broad discretion over immigration matters brought before the immigration courts and DHS, there are certain matters that the Board generally does not have the authority to review, such as:

- the length of a grant of voluntary departure granted by an immigration judge under former § 244(e) of the Immigration and Nationality Act and current § 240B of the Immigration and Nationality Act

- direct appeals from persons removed or deported in absentia pursuant to former § 242B of the Immigration and Nationality Act and current § 240(b) of the Immigration and Nationality Act

- credible fear determinations, whether made by an Asylum Officer or an immigration judge

- reasonable fear determinations made by immigration judge

- applications for advance parole

- applications for adjustment of status denied by DHS

- orphan petitions

- employment-based immigrant visa petitions

- waivers of the two-year foreign residence requirement for J-1 exchange visitors

- H and L nonimmigrant visa petitions

- K-1 fiancé/fiancée petitions

- employer sanctions

See 8 C.F.R. § 103.3, 28 C.F.R. §§ 68.53(a), 68.55.

(c) Scope of Review —

(1) Immigration judge decisions —

(A) Questions of fact — By regulation, the Board applies a clearly erroneous standard to an immigration judge's findings of fact, including credibility findings. See 8 C.F.R. § 1003.1(d)(3)(i).

(B) Questions of law — The Board applies a de novo standard of review to questions of law, discretion, judgment, and other issues. See 8 C.F.R. § 1003.1(d)(3)(ii).

(2) DHS officer decisions — The Board applies a de novo standard to all appeals of DHS officer decisions. 8 C.F.R. § 1003.1(d)(3)(iii).

(d) Board Decisions — Board decisions are rendered either by a single Board Member, by a panel of three, or in rare instances, the entire Board. See Chapter 1.3(a) (General). Upon the entry of a decision, the Board serves its decision upon the parties by regular mail, or through the EOIR Courts & Appeals System (ECAS) in eligible cases. An order issued by the Board is final, unless and until it is stayed, modified, rescinded, or overruled by the Board, the Attorney General, or a federal court. See generally 8 C.F.R. § 1003.1(d)(7), (g). An order is deemed effective as of its issuance date unless the order provides otherwise. Board decisions are generally released in one of two forms: published or unpublished. For the citation format for Board cases, see Chapter 4.6(d) (Citation).

(1) Published decisions — Published decisions are binding on the parties to the decision. Published decisions also constitute precedent that binds the Board, the immigration courts, and DHS. The vast majority of the Board's decisions are unpublished, but the Board periodically selects cases to be published. See 8 C.F.R. § 1003.1(g). DHS decisions may also be published. See 8 C.F.R. §§ 103.3(c); 1103.3(c).

(A) Criteria — Decisions selected for publication meet one or more of several criteria, including but not limited to: the resolution of an issue of first impression; alteration, modification, or clarification of an existing rule of law; reaffirmation of an existing rule of law; resolution of a conflict of authority; and discussion of an issue of significant public interest.

(B) Publication — When a decision is selected for publication, it is prepared for release to the public. Headnotes are added, and an I&N Decision citation is assigned. Where appropriate, the parties' names are abbreviated, and registration numbers (A-Numbers) are redacted. The decision is then served on the parties in the same manner as an unpublished decision.

Precedent decisions are collected and published in bound volumes of *Administrative Decisions Under Immigration and Nationality Laws of the United States* ("I&N Decisions"). Copies of individual decisions may be obtained from the Board's Internet site. See Chapter 1.6(e) (Electronic

Communications). Questions about how to obtain copies of published cases may be directed to the EOIR's library. See Chapter 1.5(b) (Library).

(C) Interim Decisions — In the past, the Board issued precedent decisions as slip opinions, called "Interim Decisions," before publication in a bound volume. See subsection (B), above. While precedent decisions are still assigned an "Interim Decision" number for administrative reasons, the proper citation is always to the volume and page number of the bound volume. See subsection (B), above. The use of the Interim Decision citation is greatly disfavored by the Board.

(2) Unpublished decisions — Unpublished decisions are binding on the parties to the decision but are *not* considered precedent for unrelated cases. Should a party in an unrelated matter nonetheless wish to refer to an unpublished Board decision, a copy of that decision should be attached to the party's brief, motion, or other submission. If a copy is not available, the last three digits of the registration number (A-Number) and full date of the Board's decision should be provided. The Board will entertain requests to publish an unpublished decision, but such requests are granted sparingly.

(3) Advisory opinion — The Board does not issue advisory opinions.

(e) Immigration Judges — As a general matter, immigration judges decide issues of removability, deportability, and admissibility, and adjudicate applications for relief. The Board has broad authority to review the decisions of immigration judges. See 8 C.F.R. § 1003.1(b). While the immigration courts and the Board are both components of EOIR, the two are separate and distinct entities. Thus, administrative supervision of immigration judges is vested in the Office of the Chief Immigration Judge, not the Board. See Chapter 1.2(c) (Relationship to the Immigration Court).

(f) Department of Homeland Security — The Department of Homeland Security (DHS) enforces the immigration and nationality laws and represents the U.S. government's interests in removal, deportation, and exclusion proceedings. DHS also adjudicates visa petitions and applications for immigration benefits. See, e.g., 8 C.F.R. § 1003.1(b)(4), (5). DHS is entirely separate from the Department of Justice. When appearing before the Board, DHS is deemed a party to the proceedings. See Chapter 1.2(d) (Relationship to the Department of Homeland Security (DHS)), Appendix B (Org Chart). The decisions of the Board are binding on DHS, unless modified or overruled by the Attorney General or a federal court. See Chapters 1.4(a) (Jurisdiction), 1.4(d) (Board Decisions).

(g) Attorney General — Decisions of the Board are reviewable by the Attorney General and may be referred to the Attorney General, at the request of the Attorney General, DHS, or the Board. The Attorney General may vacate decisions of the Board and issue their own decisions. 8 C.F.R. § 1003.1(d)(1)(i), 1003.1(h). Decisions of the Attorney General may be published as precedent decisions in *Administrative Decisions Under Immigration and Nationality Laws of the United States* ("I&N Decisions").

(h) Federal Courts — The decisions of the Board are reviewable in federal courts, depending on the nature of the appeal. When a decision of the Board is reviewed by a federal court, the Board provides that court with a certified copy of the record before the Board. The Board cannot advise parties regarding the propriety of or means for seeking judicial review. The Board is not a party before the federal courts. When Board decisions are litigated before the federal courts, the United States government is represented by the Office of Immigration Litigation (OIL) or the United States Attorney's Office. See Chapter 1.2(h) (Relationship to the Office of Immigration Litigation (OIL)). When a federal court remands a case back to the Board for further action, the Board is usually notified by the office representing the government in the proceedings before the federal court.

1.5   Public Access

(a) Office Location — The Board of Immigration Appeals (Board) is located in Falls Church, Virginia, which is within the metropolitan Washington, D.C. area. With the specific exceptions made for the public information window, and on appropriate occasions the Oral Argument Room, access to Board facilities is limited to authorized personnel.

(b) Library —

(1) Law Library and Immigration Research Center — EOIR maintains a Law Library and Immigration Research Center (LLIRC) at 5107 Leesburg Pike, Suite 1800, Falls Church, Virginia 22041. The library is located on the eighteenth floor of Skyline Tower of the Skyline complex. The library maintains select sources of immigration law, including Board decisions, federal statutes and regulations, federal case reporters, immigration law treatises, and various secondary source materials. The LLIRC serves the Board and the component agencies of EOIR but is also open to the public. For hours, directions, and collection information, contact the library at (703) 605-1103 or visit EOIR's Internet site. See Appendix A (Directory).

The LLIRC is not a lending library, and all materials must be viewed on the premises. While library staff may assist patrons in locating materials, library staff is not available for research assistance. Library staff may not provide legal advice or guidance regarding filing, procedures, or follow-up for matters before the Board or the immigration courts. Library staff may, however, provide guidance in locating published decisions of the Board. The LLIRC does not accept any filings for any individual proceedings. See Chapter 3 (Filing with the Board). Limited self-service photocopying is available in the library. Smoking is prohibited.

(2) Virtual Law Library — The LLIRC also maintains a "Virtual Law Library" accessible at EOIR's website. The Virtual Law Library serves as a comprehensive repository of immigration-related law and information for use by practitioners and the general public.

(c) Immigration Court Online Resource (ICOR) — The Immigration Court Online Resource (ICOR) is a web-based application available on EOIR's website that provides a centralized location for information and resources about immigration proceedings before EOIR. ICOR does not contain information regarding appeals from decisions made by DHS officers. See Chapter 1.4(a) (Jurisdiction).

(d) Oral Argument — The public may attend oral argument under certain circumstances. See Chapter 8 (Oral Argument).

(e) Records —

    (1) Inspection by parties — Parties to a proceeding, and their practitioners of record, may inspect the official records of proceedings. A FOIA request is not required. Inspection by prior arrangement with the Board Clerk's Office is strongly recommended to ensure that the official record of proceedings is immediately available. Parties to a proceeding before the Board may request inspection by calling the BIA Clerk's Office. See Appendix A (Directory). Parties may review all portions of the record that are not prohibited (e.g., classified information, documents under a protective order). EOIR prohibits the removal of official records by parties or other persons from EOIR-controlled spaces.

    (2) Inspection by non-parties — Persons or entities who are not party to a proceeding must file a request for information pursuant to the Freedom of Information Act (FOIA) with EOIR's Office of the General Counsel. See Chapter 13 (Requesting Records). The Clerk's Office may not permit non-parties to inspect the record or any part thereof.

    (3) Copies for parties — The Board does not automatically provide a copy of the official record of proceedings to the parties to the proceedings upon the filing of an appeal or motion. The Clerk's Office will provide copies of the official record of proceedings to parties and their practitioners of record upon request. A FOIA request is not required. Parties may obtain a copy of all portions of the record that are not prohibited (e.g., classified information, documents under a protective order). Requests for copies of the official record of proceedings may be made to the BIA in person, by mail, or by email. The Board encourages parties to request a copy by email using "EOIR.BIA.ROP.Requests@usdoj.gov". This email address is only to be used for requests for a copy of the official record. The Board does not provide self-service copying. Alternatively, the parties may file a request pursuant to the Freedom of Information Act (FOIA). See Chapter 13 (Requesting Records).

    (4) Copies for non-parties — The Clerk's Office will not provide non-parties with copies of any official record, whether in whole or in part. Non-parties must file a request for information pursuant to the Freedom of Information Act (FOIA) with EOIR's Office of the General Counsel. See Chapter 13 (Requesting Records).

    (5) Confidentiality — The Board must balance the public's need for information with the protection of persons who appear before the Board. The

Board takes special precautions to ensure the confidentiality of cases involving asylum applicants, battered noncitizen spouses and children, exclusion proceedings, and classified information.

(6) Electronic records — For cases with electronic records of proceedings (eROPs), eligible parties may view and download the eROP through ECAS, except any restricted portion of the record (e.g., classified information or information subject to a protective order).

1.6   Inquiries

(a) All Communications — All inquiries to the Board must contain or provide the following information for each respondent:

- complete name (as it appears on the charging document or petition)

- A-number, if applicable

- type of proceeding (removal, deportation, exclusion, bond, visa petition)

See also Chapter 3.3(c)(6) (Cover page and caption). If a party has more than one case before the Board, the inquiry must specify which case is the subject of the inquiry.

(b) Telephone Calls — Most questions to the Board can be answered through one of two automated phone numbers, Automated Case Information Hotline (also known as the "1-800 phone number") and "BIA TIPS". See Appendix H (Hotlines). Requests for action must be in writing unless there is an emergency situation. See generally Chapter 6 (Stays and Expedite Requests). Requests for information may be made in writing or telephonically, pursuant to the procedures set forth below. Collect calls are not accepted.

(1) Simple inquiries —

(A) Automated Case Information Hotline — The Automated Case Information Hotline provides information about the status of cases before an immigration judge or the Board. See Appendix A (Directory), Appendix H (Hotlines). The Automated Case Information Hotline contains a phone menu (in English and Spanish) covering most kinds of cases. The caller must provide the A-number of the respondent involved. A-numbers have nine digits (e.g., A234 567 890). Formerly, A-numbers had eight digits (e.g., A12 345 678). In the case of an eight-digit A-number, the caller should enter a "0" before the A-number (e.g., A012 345 678). For cases before the Board, the Automated Case Information Hotline contains information regarding:

- appeals of most immigration judge decisions

- briefing deadlines

- filing instructions

For cases before the Board, the Automated Case Information Hotline does not contain information regarding:

- bond, interlocutory, and visa petition appeals

- motions before the Board

- appeals of motions to reopen or to reconsider

- remands from a federal court to the Board

If an inquiry cannot be answered by calling the Automated Case Information Hotline, inquiries may be directed to the Clerk's Office. See Appendix A (Directory). Callers must be aware that clerks, like all Board staff, are prohibited from providing any legal advice, and that no information provided by the Clerk's Office may be construed as legal advice.

(B) BIA TIPS — The Board of Immigration Appeals Telephonic Instructions and Procedures System or "BIA TIPS" contains recorded answers to commonly asked questions, including how to file an appeal, motion, brief, change of address, or other document with the Board. See Appendix A (Directory), Appendix H (Hotlines). When the recorded information does not adequately answer the question, pressing "0" for the operator connects the caller with Clerk's Office staff.

(2) Complex inquiries — Callers must bear in mind that the Board may not engage in ex parte communications or provide legal advice. Complex inquiries are best submitted in writing, whenever possible and appropriate. In the event that a telephonic inquiry is inappropriate for the Clerk's Office, the Clerk's Office may advise a caller to submit an inquiry in writing or otherwise refer the caller to qualified personnel. See Appendix A (Directory).

(3) Projected processing times — Given the volume and the varying complexity of the cases before the Board, the Board cannot predict processing times upon request. However, most parties can expect to receive a filing receipt for an appeal, a motion to reopen, or a motion to reconsider within 1-2 weeks of filing.

(4) Inquiries to specific staff members — Because of concerns regarding ex parte communications and judicial propriety, the Board does not permit parties to communicate directly with the Board Members or other staff assigned to any given case. For this reason, the Board does not reveal to the public the names of the Board Members or other staff who are assigned to a pending case.

(5) Emergencies and expedite requests — The Board provides special procedures for emergency situations. See Chapter 6 (Stays and Expedite Requests).

(c) Faxes — The Board does not accept faxes or other electronic transmissions transmitted directly to the Board without prior authorization. Faxes that are sent to a third party and then hand-delivered to the Board are acceptable under certain circumstances. See Chapter 3.1(a)(5) (Faxes).

(d) Mail and other forms of delivery — The Board no longer uses different addresses for different means of delivery. All mail sent through the U.S. Postal Service, courier, overnight delivery, or hand-delivered items must be addressed to the Board's street address. See Appendix A (Directory). The public should carefully observe the guidelines in Chapter 3.1(a)(3) (Where to file). An "attention" line indicating the intended recipient, if the name or office is known, should appear at the bottom left of the envelope or at the appropriate location on the mailing label or form.

(e) Electronic Communications —

(1) Internet — The Executive Office for Immigration Review (EOIR) maintains an Internet web site at http://www.justice.gov/eoir. See Appendix A (Directory). The site contains information about the Board and other components of EOIR, such as newly published regulations and Board precedent decisions, events at EOIR, and a copy of this manual.

(2) EOIR Courts & Appeals System (ECAS) — The EOIR Courts & Appeals System (ECAS) is a suite of EOIR web-based applications that allows attorneys and fully accredited representatives to electronically register with EOIR, access case information and hearing calendars, as well as electronically file documents and view electronic records of proceedings (eROPs) in eligible cases. Similarly, these web-based applications provide access for authorized DHS users. Access to these applications is available on EOIR's website at https://www.justice.gov/eoir/ECAS.

(3) Electronic Registry (eRegistry) — Attorneys and fully accredited representatives who are accredited to appear before EOIR must electronically register with EOIR in order to appear before the Board. eRegistry is the online process that is used to electronically register with EOIR. See Chapter 2.1(b) (Entering an Appearance).

(4) E-mail — The Board does not correspond with the public through e-mail communications except in the following instances:

- E-mail generated through the ECAS suite of web-based applications. See subsection (2), above.

- Parties request of a copy of the official record of proceedings. See Chapter 1.5(e)(3) (Copies for parties). Note that this email address is only to be used to request a copy of the official record of proceedings.

(5) Faxes — See subsections (c), above.

(6) Automated Case Information system (ACIS) — The Automated Case Information system (ACIS) provides information about the status of cases (in English and Spanish) before immigration judges and the Board. The information on ACIS is similar to the information provided by telephone via the Automated Case Information Hotline. See Chapter 1.6(b)(1)(A) (Automated Case Information Hotline). Access to ACIS is available on EOIR's website at https://acis.eoir.justice.gov/en/.

(f) Emergencies and Expedite Requests — If imminent deportation or other impending circumstances require urgent Board action, parties should follow the procedures set forth in Chapter 6 (Stays and Expedite Requests).

Chapter 2 Appearances before the Board

2.1   Representation and Appearances Generally

(a) Right to Counsel and Individuals Authorized to Provide Representation and Make Appearances — Under the regulations, parties appearing before the Board may represent themselves (Chapter 2.2) or be represented by practitioners. See 8 C.F.R. §§ 1001.1(ff), 1292.1. Practitioners include: attorneys (Chapter 2.3), accredited representatives (Chapter 2.4), and certain kinds of individuals who are expressly recognized by the Board (Chapters 2.5 and 2.9).

If a respondent wishes to be represented, the respondent may be represented by a practitioner of their choosing, at no cost to the government. A list of pro bono legal service providers who may be willing to represent respondents at no cost is accessible on EOIR's website. The pro bono providers may represent respondents on appeal as well as in immigration court. Bar associations and nonprofit agencies can also refer respondents to practitioners.

Attorneys and fully accredited representatives who are accredited to appear before EOIR must register with EOIR's eRegistry in order to appear before the Board. See 8 C.F.R. § 1292.1(f). Other practitioners are not required to register with EOIR.

No one, other than a practitioner, is authorized to appear before the Board. Non-lawyer "immigration specialists," "visa consultants," and "notarios" are not authorized to represent parties or appear before the Board. See Chapter 2.7 (Immigration Specialists).

(b) Entering an Appearance as the Practitioner of Record — To perform the functions of and become the practitioner of record, a practitioner must file a Notice of Appearance as Attorney or Representative Before the Board of Immigration Appeals (Form EOIR-27) for each represented party on a separate Form EOIR-27. See 8 C.F.R. §§ 1003.38(g)(1), 1292.4. A practitioner of record is authorized and required to appear on behalf of a respondent, to file all documents on behalf of a respondent, and to accept service of process of all documents filed in the proceedings before the Board. See 8 C.F.R. §§ 1003.38(g)(1)(ii), 1292.5(a). A properly filed Form EOIR-27) provides a practitioner with access to the record of proceedings during the course of proceedings before the Board. See 8 C.F.R. § 1003.38(g)(1)(ii). A respondent is considered to be represented for the Board proceeding in which a Notice of Appearance (Form EOIR-27) has been properly filed and accepted. See 8 C.F.R. § 1003.38(g)(1)(ii).

A practitioner seeking to be the practitioner of record, or who is the practitioner of record, must file a Form EOIR-27 in the following situations:

- the filing of an appeal

- the filing of a motion to reopen

- the filing of a motion to reconsider

- the first appearance of a practitioner

- any change of business address for the practitioner

- request a copy of the official record of proceedings

- other motions

(1) How to File the Form EOIR-27 —

(A) Electronic Entry of Appearance — After registering with EOIR's eRegistry, attorneys and accredited representatives must electronically file a Notice of Appearance (Form EOIR-27) through ECAS in cases eligible for electronic filing. If filing an appeal or motion on paper, users may electronically file their EOIR-27, but must include a paper copy of the EOIR-27 with their appeal or motion filing.

(B) Paper Entry of Appearance — Practitioners who are neither attorneys nor accredited representatives must file a paper Notice of Appearance (Form EOIR-27) in all circumstances.

When filing a paper Form EOIR-27, practitioners must use the most current version of the form, which can be found on EOIR's website. Note that Form EOIR-27 is not the same as the appearance form used before the immigration court (Form EOIR-28), and that the Board will not recognize a practitioner using Form EOIR-28. Unrepresented persons ("pro se" respondents) should not file a Form EOIR-27.

(C) Notice to opposing party — The Notice of Appearance (Form EOIR-27) may need to be served on the Department of Homeland Security in certain circumstances. See Chapter 3.2 (Service).

(2) Scope of Representation — Once a practitioner has made an appearance as the practitioner of record through the filing of a Notice of Appearance (Form EOIR-27), the practitioner has an obligation to continue representation until such time as the respondent terminates representation, another practitioner enters an appearance on a Form EOIR-27, or a motion to withdraw as counsel has been granted by the Board. See 8 CFR 1003.38(g)(1)(iii).

(3) Change in Representation — A represented respondent may substitute or release a practitioner of record before the Board at their discretion. A practitioner of record may withdraw from representation under certain conditions. Respondents and their practitioners of record must keep the Board apprised of all changes in representation.

(A) Substitution of counsel — A represented respondent may substitute a practitioner at their discretion. When a respondent wishes to substitute a new practitioner for a previous practitioner, the new practitioner must file a Notice of Appearance (Form EOIR-27). The new practitioner is expected to serve a copy of the Form EOIR-27 on the prior practitioner as well as DHS if required. See Chapter 3.2 (Service).

Upon receipt of the new Form EOIR-27, the Board automatically recognizes the new practitioner as the practitioner of record, and the prior practitioner need not file a motion to withdraw. However, until such time as a new Form EOIR-27 has been filed, the prior practitioner remains the practitioner of record and is accountable as such.

Extension requests that are based on substitution of counsel are not favored. See Chapter 4.7(c) (Extensions).

(B) Release of counsel — A represented respondent may, at their discretion, terminate representation by a practitioner of record before the Board at any time.

If a represented respondent dismisses their practitioner of record and does not retain a new practitioner immediately, the represented respondent should notify the Board through correspondence with a cover page labeled. "NOTICE OF DISMISSAL OF PRACTITIONER." See Appendix E (Cover Pages). This "dismissal notice" should contain the full name, A-Number, and complete address of the respondent, as well as the name of the practitioner of record being dismissed. The dismissal notice should also contain Proof of Service indicating that both the practitioner of record and DHS have been served. See Chapter 3.2 (Service). An updated Change of Address Form (Form EOIR-33/BIA) should accompany the dismissal notice.

If a represented respondent dismisses one practitioner of record but retains a new practitioner who immediately files a Form EOIR-27, the respondent need not file a dismissal notice for the first practitioner of record.

If, after a dismissal notice has been filed, a respondent retains a new practitioner, the new practitioner must file a Notice of Appearance (Form EOIR-27).

(C) Withdrawal of counsel — A practitioner of record seeking withdrawal should file a motion with a cover page labeled "MOTION TO WITHDRAW AS COUNSEL." See Chapter 3.2 (Service), Appendix E (Cover Pages). The motion should contain the following information:

- the last known address of the represented respondent

- evidence that the practitioner of record has notified or attempted to notify the respondent of the request to withdraw as counsel

- evidence that either (a) the respondent is aware of pending deadlines, existing obligations, and the consequences for failing to comply with those deadlines and obligations, or (b) the practitioner of record attempted to notify the respondent of those deadlines and obligations

See *Matter of Rosales*, 19 I&N Dec. 655 (BIA 1988). Withdrawal should be effected in a timely fashion to avoid compromising the interests of the respondent.

(4) Multiple practitioners of record — — Sometimes, a respondent may retain more than one practitioner for representation before the Board. All of the practitioners seeking to appear before the Board must file a Notice of Appearance (Form EOIR-27), and each Form EOIR-27 must be annotated to reflect whether the specified practitioner is the primary or non-primary practitioner of record. Only the primary practitioner of record will receive mailings from the Board. All of the practitioners, regardless of primary or non-primary designation, are practitioners of record and are individually responsible as practitioners for the respondent. All submissions to the Board must bear the name of one of the practitioners of record and be signed by the practitioner of record whose name is on the submission. See Chapter 3.3(b) (Signatures).

Circumstances may arise that require the Board to switch service of mailings from the primary practitioner of record to a non-primary practitioner of record. For example, if the primary practitioner of record is suspended from practice before the Board and immigration courts, or a discrepancy exists as to the designation of primary and non-primary in the received Form EOIR-27s, or no designation is made by the practitioners on the received Form EOIR 27s. When discrepancies occur, the Board will make reasonable efforts to resolve the discrepancy with the practitioners. However, service of Board notices and orders will not be delayed as a result of the suspension of the primary practitioner of record, discrepancies as to designations of primary and non-primary on the Form EOIR-27s, or failure to designate the primary practitioner of record on the Form EOIR-27s. As noted above, *all* the practitioners are practitioners of record, and the Board may change the primary practitioner of record designation when warranted.

(5) Law Firms/Organizations — Only individual practitioners, and not firms, offices, or organizations, may enter an appearance before the Board. A named practitioner must enter an appearance on a Notice of Appearance (Form EOIR-27) to act as the practitioner of record. Accordingly, the Board does not accept appeals, motions, briefs, or other filings submitted by a law firm, law office, or other entity, if they do not include the name and signature of the practitioner of record. See also Chapter 3.3(b)(3) (Law firms/organizations). If at any time, more than one practitioner represents a respondent, one of the practitioners must be designated as the primary practitioner of record to receive Board notices and orders. See subsection (4) above.

(A) Change in firm/organization — In the event that a practitioner departs a law firm or organization but wishes to continue representing the respondent as the practitioner of record, the practitioner must promptly file a new Notice of Appearance (Form EOIR-27). The new Form EOIR-27 must reflect any change of address information and should apprise the Board of their change in office affiliation. The practitioner should check the "new address" box in the address block on the new Form EOIR-27. The practitioner must also update their eRegistry information online prior to submitting a new Form EOIR-27.

(B) Change in practitioner — If the practitioner of record leaves a law firm/organization but the law firm/organization wishes to retain the case, another practitioner in the firm/organization must promptly file a Notice of Appearance (Form EOIR-27) and thereby become the practitioner of record. Similarly, if a law firm/organization wishes to reassign responsibility for a case from the practitioner of record to another practitioner in the firm/organization, the new practitioner must file a Form EOIR-27. Until such time as another practitioner files a Form EOIR-27 (or a motion to withdraw is granted by the Board), the original practitioner of record remains the practitioner of record and is responsible for the case.

(6) Address Obligations of Practitioners — All practitioners have an affirmative duty to keep the Board apprised of their current contact information, including address and email address. See 8 C.F.R. §§ 1003.2(g)(9)(ii), 1003.3(g)(6)(ii), 1003.38(e). Changes in an attorney's or accredited representative's contact information should be made by updating the registration information in EOIR's eRegistry to include the new contact information. However, updates to the registration information in EOIR's eRegistry do not change an attorney's or an accredited representative's address in individual cases.

For practitioners of record, the practitioner must submit a new Notice of Appearance (Form EOIR-27) for each respondent for which the practitioner's address is being changed.. The practitioner should check the "New Address" box in the address block on the Form EOIR-27. The practitioner should not submit a change of address on the respondent's Change of Address Form (Form EOIR-33/BIA).

(A) No compound changes of address — A practitioner of record must submit a separate Notice of Appearance (Form EOIR-27) for each respondent represented. A practitioner of record may not submit a list of clients for whom their change of address should be entered.

(B) Address obligations of represented respondents — Even when a respondent is represented by a practitioner of record, the respondent is still responsible for keeping the Board apprised of their current address. Address changes by practitioners of record on behalf of their clients must be submitted through the Case Portal. Changes of address for the respondent may not be made on the Notice of Appearance (Form EOIR-27) but must be made on the Change of Address Form (Form EOIR-33/BIA). See Chapter 2.2(c) (Address Obligations).

(7) Filings After Entry of Appearance as Practitioner of Record — After a practitioner has filed a Notice of Appearance (Form EOIR-27) and become the practitioner of record, all filing and communications to the Board should be submitted through the practitioner of record. Filings should always be made by a party to the proceedings, or a party's practitioner of record, and not by a third party.

(8) No filings "on behalf of" — The Board only accepts filing by the practitioner of record, not *on behalf of* the practitioner of record. Thus, except as provided in subsection (4) regarding multiple practitioners of record, any filing from a practitioner who is not the practitioner of record *must* be accompanied by a completed Notice of Appearance (Form EOIR-27), whereupon that practitioner will become the new practitioner of record.

(c) Limited Appearance for Document Assistance — Practitioners who have not filed a Notice of Appearance (Form EOIR-27) to become the practitioner of record as discussed in section (b) above and who provide assistance to unrepresented or pro se respondents with the drafting, completion, or filling in of blank spaces of a specific appeal, motion, brief, form, or other document or set of documents intended to be filed with the Board must disclose such assistance by completing a Notice of Entry of Limited Appearance for Document Assistance Before the Board of Immigration Appeals (Form EOIR-60). See 8 C.F.R. § 1003.38(g)(2). In contrast to a practitioner of record, a practitioner who provides document assistance and discloses that assistance on a Notice of Limited Appearance (Form EOIR-60) does not have any ongoing obligations to the unrepresented or pro se respondent or the Board, if and when the Notice of Limited Appearance (Form EOIR-60) and the associated assisted documents are filed with the Board. A practitioner who enters a limited appearance is not authorized or required to appear before the Board on behalf of the unrepresented or pro se respondent, is not authorized to have access to the record of proceedings and is not required file a motion to withdraw. An unrepresented or pro se respondent who receives document assistance is not represented, remains pro se, and is subject to service of process of all documents filed in the proceedings. See 8 C.F.R. §§ 1003.38(g)(2)(ii), 1292.5.

(1) Filing Form EOIR-60 and Assisted Documents — A Notice of Limited Appearance (Form EOIR-60) is not filed as a standalone document and must be paper-filed at the same time as the document or set of documents with which the practitioner assisted. See 8 C.F.R. § 1003.38(g)(2)(i).

Practitioners should use the most current version of the Notice of Limited Appearance (Form EOIR-60), which can be found on the EOIR's website at www.justice.gov/eoir. See also Chapter 12 (Forms). Note that there is a distinction between the Board's Notice of Limited Appearance (Form EOIR-60) and the immigration court's version of the Notice of Limited Appearance (Form EOIR-61). The Board will not recognize a Form EOIR-61 filed with the Board, and assisted document or set of documents received with a Form EOIR-61 will be rejected.

The Notice of Limited Appearance (Form EOIR-60) and assisted document or set of documents may be filed by the unrepresented or pro se respondent or the unrepresented or pro se respondent may arrange for another individual, such as the practitioner who assisted, to file the documents in accordance with EOIR filing polices. See Chapter 3.1 (Delivery and Receipt). A Notice of Limited Appearance (Form EOIR-60) will not be accepted if a respondent has a practitioner of record in the relevant proceeding before the Board.

After the filing of a Notice of Limited Appearance (Form EOIR-60) and assisted document(s), any subsequent filing of an assisted document or set of documents must be accompanied by a new Notice of Limited Appearance (Form EOIR-60) from the practitioner, regardless of whether the same practitioner is providing assistance. See 8 C.F.R. § 1003.38(g)(2)(i).

(2) Practitioner Identification on Assisted Documents — Notwithstanding a practitioner's disclosure of assistance on a Notice of Limited Appearance (Form EOIR-60), the practitioner must comply with the particular disclosure requirements for preparers on applications and forms, and the practitioner must identify themselves by name, accompanied by their signature, on appeals, motions, briefs, or other documents intended to be filed with the Board pursuant to a limited appearance for document assistance. See 8 C.F.R. § 1003.38(g)(3).

(3) Limited Appearances for Document Assistance Only Permitted in Cases that Originated in the Immigration Court — Practitioners are only permitted to make a limited appearance for document assistance through a Notice of Limited Appearance (Form EOIR-60), as discussed above, in Board proceedings related to cases arising from the immigration court. Limited appearances for document assistance through the Notice of Limited Appearance (Form EOIR-60) are not permitted in cases before the Board arising from a DHS decision, such as those related to a visa petition, waivers of inadmissibility for nonimmigrants under § 212(d)(3)(A)(ii) of the Immigration and Nationality Act, or fine. Any Notice of Limited Appearance (Form EOIR-60) and the associated assisted documents filed in cases before the Board arising from a DHS decision will not be recognized and will be rejected. Practitioners that provide document assistance in such cases must file a Notice of Appearance (Form EOIR-27) as discussed above. See generally Chapters 9 (Visa Petitions), 10 (Fines).

2.2 Unrepresented Respondents ("Pro se" Appearances)

(a) Generally — An individual in proceedings may represent themselves before the Board.

Individuals may choose to be represented by a practitioner of record for their proceedings before the Board or to receive document assistance from a practitioner. See Chapter 2.1 (Representation and Appearances Generally). Due to the complexity of the immigration and nationality laws, the Board recommends that those who can obtain professional representation from a practitioner of record or document assistance from a practitioner do so. Note that document assistance before the Board from a practitioner is limited to cases that originate in the immigration court. The Board does not accept limited appearances for document assistance in cases arising from a DHS decision. See Chapter 2.1(c)(3) (Limited Appearances for Document Assistance Only Permitted in Cases that Originated in the Immigration Court).

(b) Pro Bono Program — The Board cannot give advice on when to obtain professional representation or assistance from a practitioner or whom to select. However, EOIR provides general information for persons seeking free legal services on its website. The EOIR website, through the Office of Legal Access Programs, includes information on the BIA Pro Bono Project, which matches practitioner brief writers with indigent respondents who have cases on appeal.

(c) Address Obligations — Whether represented or not, all respondents in proceedings before the Board must notify the Board within 5 business days of any change of address. See 8 C.F.R. § 1003.38(e). In all instances, the Board sends communications to the last properly provided address. If a respondent fails to keep address information up to date, the Board may treat that failure as abandonment of the respondent's appeal or motion.

(1) Form EOIR-33/BIA — Changes of address *must* be made only on Form EOIR-33/BIA. Unless the respondent is detained, *no other means of notification is acceptable*. Changes communicated through motion papers, correspondence, telephone calls, applications for relief, or other means will not be recognized, and the address information on record will not be changed. For information on obtaining or reproducing Form EOIR-33/BIA, see Chapter 12 (Forms) and Appendix D (Forms).

When submitted by an attorney or accredited representative, acting as a practitioner of record, the EOIR-33/BIA must be submitted electronically through ECAS for all cases eligible for electronic filing and in paper in all other cases. When submitted by a pro se respondent or a practitioner of record other than an attorney or accredited representative, the Form EOIR-33/BIA may be filed either in paper or electronically through the Respondent Access portal.

(2) Appeals — When an appeal is filed, the Board relies on the address for the respondent that appears in the Notice of Appeal (Form EOIR-26) until such time as a change of address is reported through the filing of a Change of Address Form (Form EOIR-33/BIA).

(3) Motions — The Board recommends that a respondent file a Change of Address Form (Form EOIR-33/BIA) whenever filing a motion to reopen, a motion to reconsider, or a motion to recalendar. This will ensure that the Board has the respondent's current address when it adjudicates the motion.

(4) Federal court remands — When the Board is notified of a federal court remand, the Board relies on the address for the respondent that was last provided to the Board. To ensure that the Board has the most current address, respondents are encouraged to file a Change of Address Form (Form EOIR-33/BIA) with the Board whenever a federal court remands their case to the Board.

(d) Address Obligations of Detained Respondents — When a respondent is detained, DHS is obligated by regulation to report to the Board any changes in the respondent's location, including where the respondent is detained and when the respondent is released. See 8 C.F.R. § 1003.19(g).

> **(1) While detained** — In recognition of the unique address problems of detained persons and to help ensure that the Board's records remain current, the Board recommends that detained persons notify the Board of their transfer from one facility or institution to another. Whenever possible, a detained respondent should report their transfer on the Change of Address Form (Form EOIR-33/BIA). See subsection (c), above.

> **(2) When released** — DHS is responsible for notifying the Board when a respondent is released from custody. 8 C.F.R. § 1003.19(g). Nonetheless, the respondent should file a Change of Address Form (Form EOIR-33/BIA) with the Board to ensure that the Board's records are current.

2.3   Attorneys

(a) Qualifications — Attorneys may represent individuals before the Board as the practitioner of record, or provide document assistance, only if they are a member in good standing of the bar of the highest court of any State, possession, territory, or Commonwealth of the United States, or the District of Columbia, and are not under any order of any court suspending, enjoining, restraining, disbarring, or otherwise restricting them in the practice of law. See 8 C.F.R. §§ 1001.1(f), 1292.1(a)(1). Any attorney appearing before the Board who is the subject of discipline in any jurisdiction must promptly notify EOIR's Office of the General Counsel. See Chapter 11.6 (Duty to Report).

> **(1) eRegistry** — Attorneys must electronically register with EOIR eRegistry through ECAS in order to appear before the Board and use ECAS. See 8 C.F.R. § 1292.1(f). An attorney who fails to provide required registration information risks being administratively suspended from practice before EOIR. Once EOIR has activated the registered account, the attorney will be assigned a unique EOIR ID number.

> **(2) Address Obligations** — All practitioners have an affirmative duty to keep the Board apprised of their current contact information, including address, email address, and telephone number. Changes in an attorney's address or contact information should be made by updating the registration information in EOIR's eRegistry to include the new address and contact information. See Chapter 2.1(b)(6) (Address Obligations of Practitioners).

(b) Appearances — Attorneys must complete the proper form to make an appearance before the Board. To perform the functions of and become the practitioner of record, the attorney must file a Notice of Appearance (Form EOIR-27) for each represented respondent. See 8 C.F.R. §§ 1003.2(g)(1), 1003.3(a)(3), 1003.38(g)(1); Chapter 2.1(b) (Entering an Appearance as the Practitioner of Record). Attorneys who have not filed a Form EOIR-27 to become the practitioner of record in a proceeding before the Board, and who provide document assistance to unrepresented or pro se respondents with the drafting, competition, or filling in the blank space of a specific appeal, motion, brief, form, or other document or set of documents intended to be filed with the Board, must disclose such assistance by completing a Notice of Limited appearance (Form EOIR-60), which must be filed along with the assisted document or set of documents. See 8 C.F.R. §§ 1003.2(g)(1), 1003.3(a)(3), 1003.38(g)(2); Chapter 2.1(c) (Limited Appearance for Document Assistance).

(1) Completing Form EOIR-27 and Form EOIR-60 — If information is omitted from the Notice of Appearance (Form EOIR-27) or Notice of Limited Appearance (Form EOIR-60), or they are not properly completed, the attorney's appearance may not be recognized, and the filing may be rejected. The following information must be completed by attorneys in completing a Form EOIR-27 or Form EOIR-60.

(A) Attorney information — The Notice of Appearance (Form EOIR-27) and Notice of Limited Appearance (Form EOIR-60) must bear an attorney's current contact information, including address, email address, and telephone number, and the attorney's signature in compliance with the requirements of Chapter 3.3(b) (Signatures). The EOIR ID number issued by EOIR through the eRegistry process *must* be provided on the Form EOIR-27 or Form EOIR-60.

(B) Bar information — When an attorney is a member of a state bar which has a state bar number or corresponding court number, the attorney *must* provide that number on the Notice of Appearance (Form EOIR-27) or Notice of Limited Appearance (Form EOIR-60). If the attorney has been admitted to more than one state bar, *each and every* state bar to which the attorney has ever been admitted – including states in which the attorney is no longer an active member or has been suspended or disbarred – must be listed and the state bar number, if any, provided.

(C) Discipline information — An attorney must not check the box regarding attorney bar membership and disciplinary action on the Notice of Appearance (Form EOIR-27) and Notice of Limited Appearance (Form EOIR-60) if the attorney is subject to an order disbarring, suspending, or otherwise restricting the attorney in the practice of law. If the attorney is subject to discipline or otherwise restricted in the practice of law, then the attorney must provide additional information on the form and may include an explanatory supplement. An attorney who fails to provide disciplinary information risks not being recognized by the Board and may be subject to disciplinary action by EOIR.

(c) Practitioner Misconduct — The Executive Office for Immigration Review has the authority to impose disciplinary sanctions upon practitioners who violate rules of professional conduct before the Board, the immigration courts, and DHS. See Chapter 11 (Discipline). Where a practitioner in a case has been suspended or disbarred from practice before the Board and the respondent has not retained new counsel, the Board will treat the respondent as pro se. All mailings from the Board, including briefing schedules and orders, will be mailed directly to the respondent. Any filing from a practitioner who has been suspended or disbarred from practice before the Board will be rejected.

2.4   Accredited Representatives

(a) Generally — A fully accredited representative is a practitioner who is not an attorney and is approved by the Assistant Director for Policy or the Assistant Director's designee to make appearances before the Board, the immigration courts, and/or DHS. A partially accredited representative is a practitioner authorized to appear solely before DHS. An accredited representative must, among other requirements, have the character and fitness to represent respondents and be employed by, or be a volunteer for, a non-profit religious, charitable, social service, or similar organization that has been recognized by the Assistant Director for Policy or the Assistant Director's designee to represent respondents. 8 C.F.R. §§ 1292.1(a)(4), 1292.11(a), 1292.12(a)-(e). Accreditation of an individual is valid for a period of up to three years, and recognition of an organization is valid for a period of up to six years. 8 C.F.R. §§ 1292.11(f), 1292.12(d). Both may be renewed. 8 C.F.R. § 1292.16.

(b) Recognized Organizations — The Assistant Director for Policy or the Assistant Director's designee, in the exercise of discretion, may recognize an eligible organization to provide representation through accredited representatives. See 8 C.F.R. § 1292.11(a); Chapter 2.2(b) (List of Pro Bono Legal Service Providers). To be recognized by EOIR, an organization must affirmatively apply for that recognition. Such an organization must establish, among other requirements, that it: is a non-profit religious, charitable, social service, or similar organization; is a Federal tax-exempt organization; has at its disposal adequate knowledge, information, and experience in immigration law and procedure; and, if the organization charges fees, has a written policy for accommodating clients unable to pay fees for immigration legal services. The qualifications and procedures for organizations seeking recognition are set forth in the regulations. 8 C.F.R. §§ 1292.11, 1292.13. A recognized organization also has reporting, recordkeeping, and posting requirements. 8 C.F.R. § 1292.14. The R&A FAQs provide responses to the most common questions about recognition. Questions regarding recognition not addressed in the R&A FAQs may be directed to the Recognition and Accreditation Program in the EOIR Office of Policy. See Appendix A (Directory).

(c) Accredited Representatives —

(1) Qualifications — Recognized organizations, or organizations applying for recognition, may request accreditation of individuals who are employed by or volunteer for that organization. The Assistant Director for Policy or the Assistant Director's designee, in the exercise of discretion, may approve accreditation of an eligible individual. No individual may apply on their own behalf. Accreditation is not transferrable from one representative to another, and no individual retains accreditation upon separation from the recognized organization. The qualifications and procedures for individuals seeking accreditation are set forth in the regulations. 8 C.F.R. §§ 1292.12, 1292.13. In addition, a fully accredited representative must register with EOIR's eRegistry in order to appear before the Board. See Chapter 2.4(c)(1)(A) (eRegistry). The R&A FAQs provide responses to the most common questions about accreditation.

(A) eRegistry — A fully accredited representative must electronically register with eRegistry through ECAS in order to appear before the Board and to use ECAS. See 8 C.F.R. § 1292.1(f). A fully accredited representative who fails to provide required registration information risks being administratively suspended from practice before EOIR. Access and instructions for eRegistry can be found on the EOIR website. Once EOIR has activated the registered account, the fully accredited representative will be assigned a unique EOIR ID number.

(B) Address Obligations — All practitioners have an affirmative duty to keep the immigration court apprised of their current contact information, including address, email address, and telephone number. Changes in an accredited representative's address or contact information should be made by updating the registration information in EOIR's eRegistry to include the new address and contact information. See Chapter 2.1(b)(6) (Address Obligations of Practitioners).

(2) Appearances — Fully accredited representatives must complete the proper form to make an appearance before the Board. To perform the functions of and become the practitioner of record, an accredited representative must file a Notice of Appearance (Form EOIR-27) for each represented respondent. See 8 C.F.R. §§ 1003.2(g)(1), 1003.3(a)(3), 1003.38(g)(1), 1292.4(a); Chapter 2.1(b) (Entering an Appearance as the Practitioner of Record). Fully accredited representatives who have not filed a Form EOIR-27 to become the practitioner of record in a proceeding before the Board and who provide document assistance to pro se respondents with the drafting, competition, or filling in the blank space of a specific appeal, motion, brief, form, or other document or set of documents intended to be filed with the Board must disclose such assistance by completing a Notice of Limited Appearance (Form EOIR-60), which must be filed along with the assisted document or set of documents. See 8 C.F.R. §§ 1003.2(g)(1), 1003.3(a)(3), 1003.38(g)(2); Chapter 2.1(c) (Limited Appearance for Document Assistance).

If information is omitted from Form EOIR-27 or Form EOIR-60, or they are not properly completed, the fully accredited representative's appearance may not be recognized, and any accompanying filing may be rejected.

(3) Immigration Specialists/Consultants — Accredited representatives should not be confused with non-lawyer immigration specialists/consultants, visa consultants, and "notarios." See Chapter 2.7 (Immigration Specialists/Consultants). Accredited representatives must be expressly accredited by the Assistant Director for Policy or the Assistant Director's designee and must be employed by or volunteer for an organization specifically recognized by the Assistant Director for Policy or the Assistant Director's designee.

(4) Verification — To verify that an individual has been accredited by EOIR, please consult the Accredited Representatives List at https://www.justice.gov/eoir/recognition-accreditation-roster-reports.

(d) Accredited Representative and Recognized Organization Misconduct — Accredited representatives and recognized organizations must comply with certain standards of professional conduct. See 8 C.F.R. § 1003.101 et seq. The Executive Office for Immigration Review has the authority to impose disciplinary sanctions upon accredited representatives and recognized organizations who violate rules of professional conduct before the Board, the immigration courts, and DHS. See Chapter 11 (Discipline of Practitioners).

(e) Request to be Removed from List of Recognized Organizations or Accredited Representatives — A recognized organization or an accredited representative who no longer wishes to be on the Recognized Organizations and Accredited Representatives Roster must submit a written request to the Recognition and Accreditation Program. See Appendix A (Directory).

2.5   Law Students and Law Graduates

(a) Generally — Law students and law graduates (law school graduates who are not yet admitted to practice law) are practitioners who may appear before the Board if certain conditions are met and the appearance is approved by the Board. Recognition by the Board is not automatic and must be requested in writing. See 8 C.F.R. § 1292.1(a)(2).

(b) Law Students —

(1) Qualifications — A law student participating in a legal aid program or clinic conducted by a law school or non-profit organization may appear in EOIR proceedings under the direct supervision of an EOIR-registered attorney or accredited representative. 8 C.F.R. § 1292.1(a)(2)(ii). The law student must not receive direct or indirect remuneration from the respondent they represent. 8 C.F.R. § 1292.1(a)(2)(ii).

(2) Appearances — The supervising attorney or accredited representative and the law student must complete the proper form, Notice of Appearance (Form EOIR-27) or Notice of Limited Appearance (Form EOIR-60), and otherwise comply with the instructions below to make an appearance before the Board. If information is omitted from Form EOIR-27 or Form EOIR-60, they are not properly completed, or the instructions below are not followed, the supervising attorney or accredited representative's and the law student's appearances may not be recognized, and any accompanying filing may be rejected.

(A) Form EOIR-27 appearance — A law student is not permitted to register with the Executive Office for Immigration Review and, therefore, cannot electronically file documents, including a Notice of Appearance (Form EOIR-27). See Chapter 2.1(b) (Entering an Appearance as the Practitioner of Record). Accordingly, the law student's supervising attorney or accredited representative must notify the Board of both individuals' appearances by filing two separate documents. The law student's supervising attorney or accredited representative must complete and submit a Form EOIR-27 as the practitioner of record in the proceeding, indicating that they are the primary practitioner. Together with that Form EOIR-27, the law student's supervising attorney or accredited representative must inform the Board of the law student's appearance by filing a "Notice of Representation by a Law Student" and a statement from the law student. The notice must include a copy of a Form EOIR-27 completed by the law student that indicates the law student's appearance is as a non-primary practitioner. The statement from the law student must indicate that the student is appearing at the request of the respondent, that the student is participating in a legal aid program or clinic conducted by a law school or non-profit organization under the direct supervision of an EOIR-registered attorney or accredited representative, and that the student is appearing without direct or indirect remuneration from the respondent they represent. C.F.R. § 1292.1(a)(2)(ii).

If the appearance is permitted by the Board, the law student will not appear as the official practitioner of record for the proceeding. Instead, the law student's supervising attorney or accredited representative is the practitioner of record for the case and the person who submits all filings on behalf of the respondent whom the law student is helping to represent. 8 C.F.R. § 1292.1(a)(2)(v). The law student's supervisor ,as the practitioner of record, is required to accompany the law student at any hearing and be prepared to proceed with the case at all times. See generally 8 C.F.R. § 1292.1(a)(2)(iv). In the Board's discretion, the law student and supervising attorney or accredited representative may appear from separate physical locations. See generally 8 C.F.R. § 1292.1(a)(2)(iv).

(B) Form EOIR-60 limited appearance for document assistance — If the law student's supervising attorney or accredited representative and the law student have not filed Notices of Appearance (Forms EOIR-27) as discussed above, and the law student provides assistance to unrepresented or pro se respondents with the drafting, completion, or filling in of blank spaces of a specific appeal, motion, brief, form, or other document or set of documents intended to be filed with the Board, the supervising attorney or accredited representative and the law student must disclose such assistance by each completing a Notice of Limited Appearance (Form EOIR-60), which must be filed along with the assisted document or set of documents. See 8 C.F.R. §§ 1003.2(g)(1), 1003.3(a)(3), 1003.38(g)(2); Chapter 2.1(c) (Limited Appearance for Document Assistance). Additionally, as above, the law student's Form EOIR-60 must be accompanied by a statement from the law student indicating that the student is appearing at the request of the unrepresented or pro se respondent, that the student is participating in a legal aid program or clinic conducted by a law school or non-profit organization under the direct supervision of an EOIR-registered attorney or accredited representative, and that the student is appearing without direct or indirect remuneration from the noncitizen.

(c) Law Graduates —

(1) Qualifications — A law graduate may appear in EOIR proceedings under the supervision of an EOIR-registered attorney or accredited representative. The law graduate must not receive direct or indirect remuneration from the respondent they represent. 8 C.F.R. § 1292.1(a)(2)(iii).

(2) Appearances — The supervising attorney or accredited representative and the law graduate must complete the proper form, Notice of Appearance (Form EOIR-27) or Notice of Limited Appearance (Form EOIR-60), and otherwise comply with the instructions below to make an appearance before the Board. If information is omitted from Form EOIR-27 or Form EOIR-60, they are not properly completed, or the instructions below are not followed, the supervising attorney's or accredited representative's and the law graduate's appearances may not be recognized, and any accompanying filing may be rejected.

(A) Form EOIR-27 appearance — A law graduate is not permitted to register with the Executive Office for Immigration Review and, therefore, cannot electronically file documents, including a Notice of Appearance (Form EOIR-27). See Chapter 2.1(b) (Entering an Appearance as the Practitioner of Record). Accordingly, the law graduate's supervising attorney or accredited representative must notify the Board of both individuals' appearances by filing two separate documents. The law graduate's supervising attorney or accredited representative must complete and submit a Form EOIR-27 as the practitioner of record in the proceeding, indicating that they are the primary practitioner. Together with that Form EOIR-27, the law graduate's supervising attorney or accredited representative must inform the Board of the law graduate's appearance by filing a "Notice of Representation by a Graduate" and a statement from the law graduate. The notice must include a copy of a Form EOIR-27 completed by the law graduate that indicates the law graduate's appearance is as a non-primary practitioner. The statement from the law graduate must indicate that the graduate is appearing at the request of the respondent, that the graduate is under the supervision of an EOIR-registered attorney or accredited representative, and that the graduate is appearing without direct or indirect remuneration from the respondent they represent. 8 C.F.R. § 1292.1(a)(2)(iii).

If the appearance is permitted by the Board, the law graduate will not appear as the official practitioner of record for the proceeding. Instead, the law graduate's supervising attorney or accredited representative is the practitioner of record for the case and the person who submits all filings on behalf of the respondent whom the law graduate is helping to represent. 8 C.F.R. § 1292.1(a)(2)(v). The law graduate's supervisor, as the practitioner of record, must accompany the law graduate at all hearings and be prepared to proceed with the case at all times. See generally 8 C.F.R. § 1292.1(a)(2)(iv). The Board may permit the law graduate and supervising attorney or accredited representative to appear from separate physical locations.

(B) Form EOIR-60 limited appearance for document assistance — If the law graduate's supervising attorney or accredited representative and the law graduate have not filed Notice of Appearances (Form EOIR-27s) as discussed above, and the law graduate provides assistance to unrepresented or pro se respondents with the drafting, completion, or filling in of blank spaces of a specific appeal, motion, brief, form, or other document or set of documents intended to be filed with the Board, the supervising attorney or accredited representative and the law graduate must disclose such assistance by each completing a Notice of Limited Appearance (Form EOIR-60), which must be filed along with the assisted document or set of documents. See 8 C.F.R. §§ 1003.2(g)(1), 1003.3(a)(3), 1003.38(g)(2); Chapter 2.1(c) (Limited Appearance for Document Assistance). Additionally, as above, the law graduate's Form EOIR-60 must be accompanied by a statement from the law graduate indicating that the graduate is appearing at the request of the unrepresented or pro se respondent, that the graduate is under the supervision of an EOIR-registered attorney or accredited representative, and that the graduate is appearing without direct or indirect remuneration from the unrepresented or pro se respondent.

(d) Practitioner Misconduct — Law students and law graduates must comply with standards of professional conduct. See 8 C.F.R. § 1003.101 et seq.

2.6   Paralegals

Paralegals are professionals who assist attorneys in the practice of law. They are not practitioners or licensed to practice law or to appear before the Board. Paralegals who do not work for an attorney risk being charged with the unauthorized practice of law.

2.7   Immigration Specialists/Consultants

Immigration specialists/consultants – who include visa consultants and "notarios" – are *not* practitioners and are not authorized to practice law or to appear before the Board. They do not qualify either as accredited representatives or "reputable individuals" under the regulations. See Chapters 2.4 (Accredited Representatives), 2.9(a) (Reputable Individuals). These individuals may be violating the law by practicing law without a license.

2.8   Family Members

If a party is a child, then a parent or legal guardian may represent the child before the Board, provided the parent or legal guardian clearly informs the Board of their relationship. If a party is an adult, a family member may represent the party *only* when the family member has been authorized by the Board to do so as a reputable individual. See Chapter 2.9(a) (Reputable Individuals).

2.9   Others

(a) Reputable Individuals — Reputable individuals are practitioners who may appear before the Board if certain conditions are met and the appearance is approved by the Board. Recognition by the Board is not automatic and must be requested in writing. See 8 C.F.R. § 1292.1(a)(3).

> **(1) Qualifications** — To qualify as a reputable individual and be permitted to appear, an individual must meet all the following criteria, as found by the Board in discretion:
>
> - be a person of good moral character
>
> - appear on an individual basis, at the request of the respondent
>
> - receive no direct or indirect remuneration for their assistance of the respondent
>
> - file a declaration that they are not being remunerated for their assistance of the respondent
>
> - have a preexisting relationship with the respondent (e.g., relative, neighbor, clergy), except in those situations where representation would otherwise not be available
>
> - be officially recognized by the Board.
>
> Any individual who receives any sort of compensation or makes immigration appearances on a regular basis (such as a non-lawyer "immigration specialist," "visa consultant," or "notario") or holds themself out to the public as qualified to do so does not qualify as a "reputable individual" as defined in the regulations.
>
> **(2) Appearances** — A reputable individual must complete the proper form, Notice of Appearance (Form EOIR-27) or Notice of Limited Appearance (Form EOIR-60), and otherwise comply with the instructions below to make an appearance before the Board. If information is omitted from Form EOIR-27 or Form EOIR-60, they are not properly completed, or the instructions below are not followed, the reputable individual's appearance may not be recognized, and any accompanying filing may be rejected. Reputable individuals are not issued EOIR ID numbers, and this part of the forms can be left blank.
>
> > **(A) Form EOIR-27 appearance** — A reputable individual is not permitted to register with the Executive Office for Immigration Review and, therefore, cannot electronically file documents, including a Notice of Appearance (Form EOIR-27). See Chapter 2.1(b) (Entering an Appearance as the Practitioner of Record). Accordingly, to appear as the practitioner of record, a reputable individual must paper file a Form EOIR-27. Together with that Form EOIR-27, the reputable individual must

include a statement demonstrating that the individual satisfies the qualification criteria in section (a)(1) above.

(B) Form EOIR-60 limited appearance for document assistance — Because of the limited circumstances in which a reputable individual is permitted to appear, a reputable individual should seek to appear as the practitioner of record through the filing of a Notice of Appearance (Form EOIR-27). However, if the reputable individual has not filed a Form EOIR-27 as discussed above, and the reputable individual provides assistance to unrepresented or pro se respondents with the drafting, completion, or filling in of blank spaces of a specific appeal, motion, brief, form, or other document or set of documents intended to be filed with the Board, the reputable individual must disclose such assistance by completing a Notice of Limited Appearance (Form EOIR-60), which must be filed along with the assisted document or set of documents. See 8 C.F.R. §§ 1003.2(g)(1), 1003.3(a)(3), 1003.38(g)(2); Chapter 2.1(c) (Limited Appearance for Document Assistance). Additionally, as above, the reputable individual's Form EOIR-60 must be accompanied by a statement from the reputable individual demonstrating that the individual satisfies the qualification criteria in section (a)(1) above.

(b) Fellow Inmates — The regulations do not provide for representation or appearances, including limited appearances for document assistance, by fellow inmates or other detained persons. Fellow inmates are not practitioners under the regulations.

(c) Accredited Officials of Foreign Government — An accredited official of a foreign government to which the respondent owes an allegiance and who is in the United States may appear before the Board as a practitioner if the appearance is in their official capacity and with the respondent's consent. See 8 C.F.R. § 1292.1(a)(5).

(1) Appearances — An accredited official must complete the proper form, Notice of Appearance (Form EOIR-27) or Notice of Limited Appearance (Form EOIR-60), and otherwise comply with the instructions below to make an appearance before the Board. If information is omitted from Form EOIR-27 or Form EOIR-60, they are not properly completed, or the instructions below are not followed, the accredited official's appearance may not be recognized, and any accompanying filing may be rejected. Accredited officials are not issued EOIR ID numbers and this part of the forms can be left blank.

(A) Form EOIR-27 appearance — An accredited official is not permitted to register with the Executive Office for Immigration Review and, therefore, cannot electronically file documents, including a Notice of Appearance (Form EOIR-27). See Chapter 2.1(b) (Entering an Appearance as the Practitioner of Record). Accordingly, to appear as the practitioner of record, an accredited official must paper file Form EOIR-27. The accredited official's Form EOIR-27 must be accompanied by evidence that the appearance is in an official capacity and that the respondent consented to the appearance.

(B) Form EOIR-60 limited appearance for document assistance — Because of the limited circumstances in which an accredited official is permitted to appear, an accredited official should seek to appear as the practitioner of record through the filing of a Notice of Appearance (Form EOIR-27). However, if the accredited official has not filed a Form EOIR-27 as discussed above and the accredited official provides assistance to unrepresented or pro se respondents with the drafting, completion, or filling in of blank spaces of a specific appeal, motion, brief, form, or other document or set of documents intended to be filed with the Board, the accredited official must disclose such assistance by completing a Notice of Limited Appearance (Form EOIR-60), which must be filed along with the assisted document or set of documents. See 8 C.F.R. §§ 1003.2(g)(1), 1003.3(a)(3), 1003.38(g)(2); Chapter 2.1(c) (Limited Appearance for Document Assistance). Additionally, the accredited official's Form EOIR-60 must be accompanied by evidence that the appearance is in an official capacity and that the unrepresented or pro respondent consented to the appearance.

(d) Former Employees of the Department of Justice — Former employees of the Department of Justice may be restricted in their ability to appear before the Board. See 8 C.F.R. § 1292.1(c).

(e) Foreign Student Advisors — A foreign student advisor is not a practitioner and is not authorized to appear before the Board unless the advisor is an accredited representative. See Chapter 2.4 (Accredited Representatives).

2.10   Amicus Curiae

The Board may grant permission to an amicus curiae to appear, on a case-by-case basis, where it serves the public interest. 8 C.F.R. § 1292.1(d). The decision to grant or deny a request to appear as amicus curiae is within the sole discretion of the Board. An appearance as amicus curiae is not a request to represent or provide document assistance to a party before the Board. Therefore, neither the Notice of Appearance (Form EOIR-27) or Notice of Limited Appearance (Form EOIR-60) is required. See Chapter 2.1 (Representation and Appearances Generally).

The Board generally limits the appearance of amicus curiae to the filing of briefs. See Chapter 4.6(i) (Amicus Curiae Briefs). Amicus curiae may request an opportunity to present oral argument, but such requests are granted sparingly. See Chapter 8.7(e)(13) (Amicus curiae).

A person or organization wishing to make an appearance as an amicus curiae must file a written request with the Clerk's Office, preferably with a cover page labeled "REQUEST TO APPEAR AS AMICUS CURIAE." See Appendix A (Directory), Appendix E (Cover Pages). That request should specify the name and A-Number of the matter in which an amicus curiae wishes to appear and articulate why amicus curiae should be permitted to appear. A brief should accompany the request to appear as amicus curiae. If the Board grants the request, the parties will be provided an opportunity to respond. See Chapter 4.6(h) (Reply Briefs), 4.6(i) (Amicus Curiae

Briefs). The request and brief should be served on all parties to the proceedings.
See Chapter 3.2 (Service).

The Board may, at its discretion, acknowledge helpful amicus curiae brief(s) and contributors.

Chapter 3 Filing with the Board

3.1   Delivery and Receipt

(a) Filing — Most appeals and motions adjudicated by the Board are filed directly with the Board. Some appeals and motions, however, are filed with DHS. See Chapters 4.2(b) (Filing), 5.2 (Filing a Motion), 7.3(a) (Filing), 9.3(c)(2) (Where to file), Appendix J (Filing Motions). No appeal, motion, correspondence, or other filing intended for the Board should ever be filed with an immigration court.

(1) Receipt rule — For appeals and motions that must be filed with the Board, the appeal or motion is not deemed "filed" until it is *received* at the Board. An electronic filing that is accepted by the Board will be deemed filed on the date it was submitted. See 8 C.F.R. § 1001.1(dd). A paper filing that is accepted by the Board will be deemed filed on the date it was received by the Board. Id. A filing that is rejected by the Board as an improper filing will not be deemed filed on the date it was submitted or received. The Board does not observe the "mailbox rule." Accordingly, receipt by any other entity – be it the U.S. Postal Service, commercial courier, or detention facility – does *not* suffice. See Chapter 1.5(a) (Office Location), Appendix A (Directory).

(2) Postage problems — All required postage or shipping fees must be paid *by the sender* before an item will be accepted by the Board. The sender is responsible for paying the proper postage in all instances. When using a courier or similar service, the sender is responsible for properly completing the packing slip, including the label and the billing information. The Board therefore rejects mailings for which the required postage has not been paid or the courier billing information has not been properly completed. See Chapter 3.1(c)(1) (Meaning of "rejected").

(3) Where to file — All paper filings to the Board must be sent to the following street address:

Board of Immigration Appeals
Clerk's Office
5107 Leesburg Pike, Suite 2000
Falls Church, VA 22041

The Board no longer uses different addresses for different means of delivery. All mail sent through the U.S. Postal Service, courier, overnight delivery, or hand-delivered items must be addressed to the street address above. See Appendix A (Directory).

An "attention" line indicating the intended recipient, if the name or office is known, should appear at the bottom left of the envelope or at the appropriate location on the mailing label or form. Parties must use the correct postage on all items mailed to the Board. See subsection (2), above. The Board will not pay postage due, and the U.S. Postal Service will return any item with insufficient postage to the sender.

Given the importance of timely filing, the Board encourages parties to use courier and overnight delivery services, whenever appropriate. However, the failure of a courier or overnight delivery service does not excuse parties from meeting filing deadlines. See Chapter 3.1(b)(4) (Delays in delivery).

(4) Separate envelopes — Unrelated cases should not be sent in one envelope. To avoid confusion, each case should either be sent separately or, if mailed as a package, in its own envelope within that package.

(5) Faxes —

(A) Sent directly to the Board — The Board does not accept facsimiles ("faxes") without prior authorization. Unauthorized transmissions are discarded without consideration of the document or notice to the sender. Faxes transmitted directly to the Board will be accepted only when solicited *by the Board* in emergencies and other compelling circumstances. See generally Chapter 6 (Stays and Expedite Requests). Faxes must be sent to the attention of the person at the Board who authorized the fax.

(B) Sent through a third party — Faxes that are sent to a third party, such as a local practitioner or a local delivery agent, and then hand-delivered to the Board are acceptable under the following conditions:

- the original document must bear an original signature

- the original document must be available to the Board upon request

- the fax copy must be legible

- the filing must clearly reflect that the submission comes from the practitioner of record or the party to the proceeding, not the practitioner receiving the fax or the agent who is delivering it

- fax header information will not be used to identify the filing party, the nature of the submission, or the timeliness of the submission

- the filing party is always responsible for the filing's legibility and timeliness

Signatures are discussed at Chapter 3.3(b) (Signatures).

(6) Electronic filing through ECAS — Electronic filing through ECAS is mandatory for attorneys and accredited representatives appearing as practitioners of record, as well as for DHS, in every case eligible for electronic filing. Further instructions regarding the content and formatting for electronically filed documents is available in the ECAS User Manual.

(b) Must be "Timely" — The Board places a date stamp on all paper filings received by the Clerk's Office. See Appendix A (Directory). Similarly, all electronic filings through ECAS receive a watermark and date stamp when successfully uploaded. Absent persuasive evidence to the contrary, the Board's date stamp is controlling in the computation of whether a filing is "timely." Because paper filings are date-stamped upon arrival at the Board, the Board strongly recommends that parties filing in paper should file as far in advance of the deadline as possible and, whenever possible, use overnight delivery couriers (such as Federal Express, United Parcel Service, DHL, etc.) to ensure timely receipt. More information on electronic filing through ECAS may found in the ECAS User Manual available on EOIR's website.

(1) Construction of "day" — All due dates at the Board are calculated in calendar days. Thus, unless otherwise indicated, all references to "days" in this manual refer to calendar days, not business days.

(2) Computation of time — For purposes of computing appeal and motion deadlines, time is measured from the date of the decision (or the mailing date of the decision, if later) to the date that the appeal or motion is received by the Board.

When counting days, the day that the decision is made (or mailed) counts as "day 0." The day after the date the decision is made (or mailed) counts as "day 1." Because the Board uses calendar days to calculate deadlines, Saturdays, Sundays, and legal holidays *are* counted toward the computation of a deadline. If, however, a deadline date falls on a weekend or a legal holiday, the deadline is construed to fall on the next business day.

(3) Specific deadlines — Specific deadlines for specific types of filings are discussed elsewhere. See Appendix C (Deadlines).

(4) Delays in delivery — Postal or delivery delays do not affect existing deadlines, nor does the Board excuse untimeliness due to such delays, except in rare circumstances. Parties should anticipate all Post Office and courier delays, whether the paper filing is made through first class mail, priority mail, or any overnight or other guaranteed delivery service. Delays caused by incorrect postage or mailing error by the sending party do not affect existing deadlines. See Chapter 3.1(a)(2) (Postage problems).

(5) ECAS system outages —

(A) Electronic filing — System outages may occur that make electronic filing through ECAS unavailable and may impact filing deadlines. Planned system outages will not impact filing deadlines since these can be proactively addressed by the parties. If EOIR determines that an unplanned outage has occurred, filing deadlines that occur on the last day for filing in a specific case will be extended until the first day of system availability that is not a Saturday, Sunday, or legal holiday. EOIR will maintain an ECAS Outage Log that will note planned and unplanned ECAS system outages.

(B) Electronic payment — If the EOIR Payment Portal is unavailable due to a Pay.gov outage which results in an untimely filing, users should explain any such outage in their motion to accept untimely filing.

(6) Natural or manmade disasters — Natural or manmade disasters may occur that create unavoidable filing delays. Parties wishing to file untimely documents after a disaster must file a motion asking the Board to accept untimely filing. See Chapter 3.1(c)(3) (Untimely). Parties must include documentary evidence to support their motion, including such evidence as affidavits and declarations under the penalty of perjury. The Board will consider each motion on a case-by-case basis.

(7) Effect of extension requests — All deadlines must be met. A pending extension request does not excuse a party from meeting a filing deadline. Unopposed requests are not automatically granted. Extensions must be affirmatively granted before a filing will be accepted past the original deadline. See Chapters 4.5 (Appeal Deadlines), 4.7(c) (Extensions).

(c) Defective Filings —

(1) Meaning of "rejected" — When the Board "rejects" a paper filing, the filing is returned to the sender with a rejection notice explaining why the filing was rejected. Similarly, when the Board "rejects" an electronic filing through ECAS, the filer receives an electronic rejection notice explaining why the filing was rejected. The term "rejected" means that the filing is defective, and the Board cannot consider the filing. It is not an adjudication of the filing or a decision regarding its content.

(2) Improperly filed — If an appeal, motion, or brief is not properly filed, it is rejected by the Clerk's Office and returned to the party with an explanation for the rejection. A filing that is rejected by the Board as an improper filing is not deemed filed on the date it was submitted or received. See 8 C.F.R. § 1001.1(dd). Parties wishing to correct the defect and refile after a rejection must do so by the original deadline, unless an extension is expressly granted by the Board. See Chapter 4.5(b) (Extensions), 4.7(c) (Extensions), 5.3 (Motion Limits). The most common reasons for rejecting an appeal or motion are (A) failure to pay a fee or submit a fee waiver application when a fee is required, and (B) failure to submit a proof of service on the opposing party, which is always required. See Chapters 3.2 (Service), 3.4 (Filing Fees), Appendix F (Cert. of Service).

(3) Untimely — If an appeal is untimely, the appeal is dismissed. See 8 C.F.R. §§ 1003.1(d)(2)(i)(G), 1003.38(b). If a motion is untimely, the motion is denied. See 8 C.F.R. § 1003.2(b)(2), (c)(2). If a brief is untimely, it is rejected and returned to the party with an explanation for the rejection. Parties wishing to refile an untimely brief must file a motion asking the Board to accept the untimely brief and attach the original submission. See Chapter 4.7(d) (Untimely Briefs).

Parties must include documentary evidence to support their motion, including such evidence as affidavits and declarations under the penalty of perjury.

(d) Filing Receipts — The Board issues receipts for certain filings. Whether or not a receipt is issued, however, parties are encouraged to obtain and retain corroborative documentation of delivery, such as mail delivery receipts and courier tracking information. (As a precaution against loss, parties should also keep copies of all items sent to the Board.)

(1) Receipt issued — The Board routinely issues receipts only for Notices of Appeal (Form EOIR-26), motions to reopen, and motions to reconsider. A receipt is not an adjudication of timeliness or a determination that a filing falls within the Board's jurisdiction, but an acknowledgment that a filing has been received by the Board. Parties who electronically file through ECAS will receive electronic notification upon successful upload and when the filing is added to the electronic record of proceedings. This electronic notification is not an adjudication of timeliness or a determination that filing is within the Board's jurisdiction.

If a filing receipt is not received within approximately two weeks, parties may call the Automated Case Information Hotline or visit the online EOIR Automated Case Information System for current information on appeals or contact the Clerk's Office for current information on appeals or motions. See Appendix A (Directory).

(2) Receipt not issued — A receipt is not issued for filings other than Notices of Appeals, motions to reopen, and motions to reconsider. The Board does not provide written receipts for other motions, briefs, or memoranda. See Chapter 4.7(b) (Processing). However, parties who electronically file through ECAS will receive electronic notification upon successful upload and when the filing is accepted and added to the electronic record of proceeding. Such electronic notifications are not an adjudication of timeliness or a determination on a motion or request.

(3) Conformed copies — When a filing arrives at the Clerk's Office, a time-and-date stamp is placed on the filing. If a filing party desires a "conformed copy" (i.e., a copy of the filing bearing the Board's time-and-date stamp), the original must be accompanied by an accurate copy of the filing, prominently marked "CONFORMED COPY; RETURN TO SENDER." The filing must also contain a self-addressed stamped envelope or comparable return delivery packaging. The Board does not return conformed copies without a prepaid return envelope or packaging. If a case has an eROP, ECAS users may download electronic copies of filings with watermarked time-and-date stamps through ECAS.

3.2   Service

(a) Service Requirement — The requirement to serve documents on the opposing party depends on whether both parties are participating in ECAS, as explained below. See 8 C.F.R. §§ 1003.2(g)(9), 1003.3(g)(6).

(1) ECAS completes service — If all parties are using ECAS in a specific case, the parties do not need to separately serve any electronically filed documents on the opposing party. Rather, the ECAS system will automatically send service notifications to both parties that a new document has been filed. The parties must continue to include a certificate of service with their electronic filing, but simply note in the certificate that service was completed through ECAS.

For purposes of ECAS service, DHS is always considered to be participating in ECAS. Conversely, when DHS is electronically filing, EOIR will provide a notification to DHS users in the DHS Portal as to whether the opposing party is participating in ECAS or requires separate service outside of the ECAS system.

(2) Separate service required — If one or more parties is not using ECAS in a specific case, then the parties must complete service separately outside of the ECAS system.

If separate service is required, a party must:

- provide, or "serve," a copy on the opposing party (or, if the party is represented, the party's practitioner of record), *and*

- declare, in writing, that a copy has been served on the opposing party (or, if the party is represented, the party's practitioner of record)

For a respondent in proceedings, the opposing party is the Department of Homeland Security (DHS). In most instances, a DHS Chief Counsel or a specific Assistant Chief Counsel is the designated officer to receive service. The opposing party is *never* the Board or the immigration judge.

This written declaration is called a "Proof of Service," which is also referred to as a "Certificate of Service." See subsection (d), below, and Appendix F (Cert. of Service). See also 8 C.F.R. §§ 1003.2(g)(1), 1003.3(a)(1), 1003.3(c).

(b) Method of Service — Service may be accomplished electronically, by hand or by mail. Paper service is complete upon hand delivery of papers to a responsible person at the address of the person being served or upon the mailing of the papers.

(c) Timing of Service — The Proof of Service must bear the actual date of transmission and accurately reflect the means of transmission (e.g., electronic, regular mail, hand delivery, overnight courier, or delivery). In all instances, service must be calculated to allow the other party sufficient opportunity to act upon or respond to the served material.

(d) Proof of Service — An appeal or motion, and all subsequent filings in support of an appeal or motion, must be accompanied by Proof of Service on the opposing party. See Appendix F (Cert. of Service). Some forms, such as the Notice of Appeal (Form EOIR-26), contain a Certificate of Service, which functions as a Proof of Service. The Board rejects any submission that is filed without Proof of Service on the opposing party. See Chapter 3.1(c)(1) (Meaning of "rejected"). The only exception is a motion that is agreed upon by all parties and jointly filed (because both parties are presumed to have seen the motion they are filing together).

A Proof of Service must specify the following:

- the name or title of the party served

- the precise and complete address of the party served

- the date of service

- the means of service (e.g., electronic, 1st class mail, overnight delivery, hand-delivery, etc.)

- the document or documents being served

- the name of the person serving the document

Every Proof of Service must be signed by the person serving the document. The Proof of Service need not be signed by the party but may be signed by someone designated by the party. In contrast, the document(s) being served must be signed by the individual who drafted or prepared the documents, whether DHS, an unrepresented or pro se respondent, a practitioner of record, or a practitioner who drafted, completed, or prepared the document(s) pursuant to a limited appearance for document assistance. See Chapter 3.3(b) (Signatures).

If service is being completed through ECAS, the Proof of Service should state, "This document was electronically filed through ECAS and both parties are participating in ECAS. Therefore, no separate service was completed."

(e) Practitioner of Record and Service —

(1) Service upon a practitioner of record — Service upon a practitioner of record constitutes service upon the person or entity represented. See 8 C.F.R. § 1292.5(a).

(2) Service by a represented respondent — The Board recommends that, whenever a respondent is represented, the respondent allow their practitioner of record handle a filing with the Board. See Chapter 2.1(b)(7) (Filings After Entry of Appearance as Practitioner of Record). If, however, a represented respondent wishes to file a document without the assistance of their practitioner of record, the respondent should serve copies of that document on both DHS and the practitioner of record, with a separate Proof of Service for each. See subsection (d), above.

(3) Service by an unrepresented respondent who received document assistance from a practitioner — An unrepresented or pro se respondent who received document assistance from a practitioner (or the designee listed on the Proof of Service) must serve the DHS with the completed Notice of Limited Appearance (Form EOIR-60) and assisted document or set of documents.

(f) Proof of Service and the Notice of Appearance — All filings with the Board must include a Proof of Service that identifies the item being filed. See subsection (d), above. Thus, the completed Proof of Service on a Notice of Appearance (Form EOIR-27) or a Notice of Limited Appearance (Form EOIR-60) by itself is *not* considered sufficient proof of service of documents accompanying the Form EOIR-27 or Form EOIR-60.

3.3   Documents

(a) Language — All Notices of Appeal (Form EOIR-26) must be submitted in the English language or be accompanied by a certified English translation. 8 C.F.R. § 1003.3(a)(3).

All motions and documentation filed in support of an appeal or motion must either be in the English language or be accompanied by an English language translation and a certification signed by the translator, printed or typed, in accordance with the regulations. See 8 C.F.R. § 1003.2(g)(1). Such certification must include a statement that the translator is competent to translate the language of the document and that the translation is true and accurate to the best of the translator's abilities. See 8 C.F.R. § 1003.33. See also Appendix G (Cert. of Translation).

(b) Signatures — No appeal, motion, brief, or request for Board action is properly filed without a signature of the individual who drafted or prepared the document(s), whether DHS, an unrepresented or pro se respondent, a practitioner of record, or a practitioner who drafted, completed, or prepared the document(s) pursuant to a limited appearance for document assistance. See 8 C.F.R. §§ 1003.38(g)(3), 1003.2(g)(8), 1003.3(g)(5). A Proof of Service also requires a signature but may be signed by someone designated by the filing party. See Chapter 3.2(d) (Proof of Service). Reproductions of signatures are acceptable when contained in a photocopy or fax of an original document as long as the original is available to the Board upon request. See subsection (d), below. See also Chapter 3.1(a) (Filing).

A signature represents a certification by the signer that: the signer has read the document; to the best of the signer's knowledge, information, and belief formed after reasonable inquiry, the document is grounded in fact; the document is submitted in good faith; and the document has not been filed for any improper purpose. See 8 C.F.R. § 1003.102(j)(1). A signature represents the signer's authorization, attestation, and accountability.

Every handwritten signature written in ink must be accompanied by a typed or printed version of the name.

(1) Paper submissions — The Board accepts handwritten ink, encrypted digital signature, or electronic signatures, subject to any form or application requirements. Reproductions of signatures *are* acceptable when contained in a photocopy or fax of an original document as long as the original is available to the Board upon request. See subsection (d), below. See also Chapter 3.1(a) (Filing).

(2) Electronic submissions — For electronic filings through ECAS, the Board accepts ink, encrypted digital signature, or electronic signatures, subject to any form or application requirements. For documents electronically filed through ECAS, a user who is logged in and electronically filing through ECAS may use a conformed signature wherever their personal signature is required. CONFORMED SIGNATURE EXAMPLE: /S/ John Doe. See 8 C.F.R. §§ 1003.38(g)(3), 1003.2(g)(8), 1003.3(g)(5). When a Notice of Appearance (Form EOIR-27) is electronically submitted, the electronic acknowledgment and submission of the Form EOIR-27 constitutes the signature of the respondent's practitioner of record.

(3) Law firms/organizations — Only the practitioner of record – not a law firm, law office/organization, or other practitioner – may sign a submission to the Board. See Chapters 2.1(b) (Entering an Appearance as the Practitioner of Record), 2.1(b)(4) (Multiple Practitioners of Record), 2.1(b)(5) (Law Firms/Organizations).

(4) Accredited representatives — Accredited representatives must sign their own submissions.

(5) Paralegals and other staff — Paralegals and other staff are not authorized to practice before the Board and may not sign a submission to the Board. See Chapter 2.6 (Paralegals). However, paralegals may sign a Proof of Service when authorized by the filing party. See Chapter 3.2(d) (Proof of Service).

(6) Other practitioners — Only those individuals who have been authorized by the Board to make appearances and have submitted a Notice of Appearance (Form EOIR-27) or Notice of Limited Appearance (Form EOIR-60) may sign submissions to the Board. See Chapters 2.5 (Law Students and Law Graduates), 2.9 (Others). Non-lawyer "immigration specialists/consultants," "notarios," and "visa consultants" are not authorized to represent a party or appear before the Board. See Chapter 2.7 (Immigration Specialists/Consultants).

(7) Family members — A family member may sign submissions on behalf of a party only under certain circumstances. See Chapter 2.8 (Family Members).

(c) Format — The Board prefers all filings and (where appropriate) supporting documents to be typed or printed, but will accept handwritten filings. The filing party should make sure that items submitted to the Board are legible.

The Board does not accept electronic media (e.g., CDs, DVDs, VHS tapes, audio cassette tapes, thumb drives, or other electronic medium). Where possible, the Board will return electronic media to the sender. The Board also does not accept faxes or other electronic transmissions without prior authorization by the Board. See Chapter 3.1(a)(5) (Faxes).

(1) Order of documents — Filings should be assembled as follows. All forms should be filled out completely.

(A) Appeals — An appeal package should comply with the instructions on the Notice of Appeal (Form EOIR-26). The appeal package should contain (in order):

1. filing fee (if applicable, stapled to the Notice of Appeal) or fee receipt (if fee paid electronically)

2. Notice of Appeal (Form EOIR-26) (with its Certificate of Service completed)

3. Fee Waiver Request (Form EOIR-26A, if unable to pay the filing fee)

4. Notice of Appearance (Form EOIR-27), or Notice of Limited Appearance (Form EOIR-60), if required

5. supporting documentation (if any)

See Chapters 2.1 (Representation and Appearances Generally), 3.2(d) (Proof of Service), 3.4 (Filing Fees), 4.4 (Filing an Appeal).

(B) Motions — A motion package should contain (in order):

1. filing fee (if applicable, stapled to the cover page of the motion) or fee receipt (if paid electronically)

2. motion (with appropriate cover page)

3. supporting documentation (if any)

4. Fee Waiver Request (Form EOIR-26A, if unable to pay the filing fee)

5. Notice of Appearance (Form EOIR-27), or Notice of Limited Appearance (Form EOIR-60), if required

6. Change of Address (Form EOIR-33/BIA, which is recommended even if the respondent's address has not changed)

7. Proof of Service

See Chapters 2.1 (Representation and Appearances Generally), 3.2(d) (Proof of Service), 3.3(c)(6) (Cover page and caption), 3.4 (Filing Fees), 5.1(b) (Practitioners), 5.2 (Filing a Motion).

(C) Supplementary filings — The Board accepts supplementary filings only in limited situations. See, e.g., Chapter 4.6(g) (Supplemental briefs). A supplementary filing should contain (in order):

1. supplementary filing (with cover page and caption)

2. supporting documentation

3. Notice of Appearance (Form EOIR-27) for a new appearance or Notice of Limited Appearance (Form EOIR-60), if required.

4. Proof of Service

See also Chapters 2.1 (Representation and Appearances Generally), 3.2(d) (Proof of Service), 3.3(c)(6) (Cover page and caption).

(2) Number of copies — Only the *original* of each appeal or motion need be filed with the Board. Similarly, only one set of supporting documents need be filed with the Board. Multiple copies of any appeal, motion, or supporting document should not be filed, unless otherwise instructed. Where there is a consolidated proceeding, only one copy need be filed for the entire group. See Chapters 4.6(e) (Consolidated Briefs), 4.10(a) (Consolidated Appeals).

(3) Number of pages — Briefs and other submissions should *always* be paginated. Parties must limit the body of their briefs to 50 pages unless otherwise directed by the Board. In computing the length limit, headings, footnotes, and quotations count toward the limit. In addition, regardless of the descriptive heading, the page count toward the page limit includes any statement of facts and procedural history, statement of issues presented for review, standard of review, summary of the argument, argument, and conclusion. By contrast, the following items do not count toward the page limit:

- cover page;

- table of contents;

- table of citations;

- signature block;

- certificate / proof of service;

- addendum containing statutes, rules, regulations, or case law; and

- supporting documentation.

Oversized briefs unnecessarily burden the Board. Motions to accept briefs that exceed the page limitation established by the Board are disfavored and will not be granted absent a showing of extraordinary and compelling circumstances. If a party files an oversized brief, the brief should be accompanied with a written motion entitled "MOTION TO EXTEND PAGE LIMIT" that generally complies with the rules and procedures for motions and filings.

See Chapter 3 (Filing with the Board), Chapter 5.2 (Filing a Motion). Thus, the motion and brief need to be submitted together. If an oversized brief is filed without a motion to extend the page limit, the brief will be rejected.

Motions to extend the page limit also should include a statement of reasons for exceeding the page limitation that demonstrates extraordinary and compelling reasons. Note that stating that a case involves asylum law or complex legal issues is not sufficient. If the motion is granted, the motion and brief are incorporated into the record, and the brief is considered by the Board. If the motion is denied, the motion is retained as part of the record, but the brief is removed without consideration. In either case, the parties are notified of the Board's decision. Motions to reconsider denials will not be considered.

(4) Paper size and quality — All documents should be submitted on standard 8 ½" x 11" paper, in order to fit into the record of proceedings. See 8 C.F.R. § 1003.32(b). Use of legal-size paper (8½" x 14") is discouraged, as is paper of other sizes. See subsection (10), below.

Paper should be of standard stock – white, opaque, and unglazed. Given its fragility and its tendency to fade, photo-sensitive facsimile paper should never be used. Ink should be dark, preferably black.

Briefs and motions should be one-sided. Supporting documentation should also be one-sided.

(5) Tabs — For paper filings, parties are strongly encouraged to use paper separators (i.e., a piece of paper with "Tab A" printed on it) instead of indexing tabs to separate the distinct portions of an appeal or motion package. Paper separators allow the Board to more easily scan the documents into the eROP. Because immigration courts generally refer to court exhibits by number, the Board prefers that parties refer to paper separators alphabetically to avoid confusion.

(6) Cover page and caption — All motions, briefs, and supplemental filings should include a cover page. The cover page should include a caption and contain the following information:

- the name and address of the filing party

- the title of the filing (such as "RESPONDENT'S MOTION TO REOPEN" or "DHS BRIEF ON APPEAL")

- the full name for each respondent covered by the filing (as it appears on the charging document)

- the A-number for each respondent covered by the filing

- the type of proceeding involved (such as removal, deportation, exclusion, bond, visa petition)

See Appendix E (Cover Pages). If the filing involves special circumstances, that information should appear prominently on the cover page, preferably in the top right corner and highlighted (e.g., "DETAINED," "EXPEDITE REQUEST," "JOINT MOTION").

(7) Fonts and spacing — Font and type size must be easily readable. "Times New Roman 12 point" font is preferred. Double-spaced text and single-spaced footnotes are also preferred. Both proportionally spaced and monospaced fonts are acceptable.

(8) Binding — The immigration courts and the Board use a two-hole punch system to maintain paper files. The Board appreciates receiving briefs and materials pre-punched with two holes along the top (centered and 2¾" apart). Submissions should neither be bound on the side nor commercially bound, as such items must be disassembled to fit into the record of proceedings and might be inadvertently damaged in the process. Submissions may be stapled in the top left corner. The use of removable binder clips is unacceptable. The use of ACCO-type fasteners is discouraged.

(9) Forms — Forms should be completed in full and must comply with certain requirements. See Chapter 12 (Forms). See also Appendix D (Forms).

(10) Photographs, original documents and odd-sized documents — The Board recommends that parties not submit original photographs or other original documents unless instructed to do so. See subsection (d), below. If a party nonetheless wishes to submit a photograph, the party should: print identifying information on the back of the photograph, including the respondent's name and A-number, display the photograph on an 8½" x 11" sheet of paper, and print the same identifying information on the sheet of paper as well.

The Board also discourages the submission of other odd-sized materials, such as official certificates, and strongly advises that parties submit photocopies. See Chapter 3.3(d)(4) (Supporting documents). If a party nonetheless wishes to submit an odd-sized document, the document should be prepared in the same way as a photograph. The Board will not accept odd-sized materials submitted on electronic media. See subsection (c) above.

(d) Originals and Reproductions —

(1) Notices of Appeal — The original Notice of Appeal (Form EOIR-26) must always bear the original signature of the person filing the appeal or, if applicable, that of that person's practitioner of record or that of the practitioner who drafted, completed, or prepared the Notice of Appeal (Form EOIR-26) pursuant to a limited appearance for document assistance. See Chapter 3.3(b) (Signatures). A copy of a signed original is acceptable, provided that the signed original is available to the Board upon request. See Chapter 3.1(a) (Filing).

(2) Motions — The original of a motion must always bear an original signature. See Chapter 3.3(b) (Signatures). A copy of a signed original is acceptable, provided that the signed original is available to the Board upon request. However, a Notice of Appeal (Form EOIR-26) *may* not be used to file a motion.

(3) Forms — The original of a form must always bear a signature. See Chapter 3.3(b) (Signatures), 12.3 (Submitting Completed Forms).

(4) Supporting documents — The Board strongly recommends that parties submit copies of supporting documents, not originals, unless instructed otherwise. The Board does not accept electronic media (e.g., CDs, DVDs, VHS tapes, audio cassette tapes, thumb drives, or other electronic medium) in place of original supporting documents. See Chapter 3.3(c) (Format). Parties should retain original documents in the event that an immigration judge or the Board requests them at a later date. The Board does not as a practice return original documents, nor can the Board ensure the return of any original documents submitted to it.

All reproductions should be clear, legible, and made on standard-sized paper. See Chapter 3.3(c)(4) (Paper size and quality). Photographs, illustrations, and tables may be reproduced by any method that results in a good copy of the original, but not by electronic media. See Chapter 3.3(c) (Format). The Board prefers that all documents, unless voluminous, be one-sided.

Parties wishing to submit original photographs, certificates, or other odd-sized documents should consult Chapter 3.3(c)(10) (Photographs, original documents, and odd-sized documents).

(e) Source Materials — When a party relies on a source of law that is not readily and publicly available free of charge, a copy of that source of law *must* be provided to the Board and the other party. When a party relies upon any supporting document, a copy of that document *must* be provided to the Board and the other party.

(1) Source of law — When a party relies on a source of law that is not readily available, that source of law should be reproduced in or attached to the brief. Similarly, if citation is made to governmental memoranda, legal opinions, advisory opinions, communiques, or other ancillary legal authority or source, copies of such items should be provided by the citing party, along with the brief.

(2) Source of factual information — Photocopied secondary source material filed in support of an appeal or motion must be clearly marked and have identifying information, including the precise title, date, and page of the material being provided. The Board strongly encourages the submission of title pages containing identifying information for the published matter (e.g., author, year of publication). Identifying information should appear on the document itself and not just in a list of exhibits or table of contents. Any copy of the State Department Country Reports on Human Rights Practices must indicate the year of that particular report.

Regarding the propriety of submitting evidence, see Chapter 4.8 (Evidence on Appeal).

(3) Highlighting — When a party submits voluminous secondary source material, that party should flag and emphasize the pertinent passages of that secondary source material, as well as specific references to a party. Additionally, a party is encouraged to use pin cites to pertinent passages when referring to that secondary source material within a brief or motion.

(f) Federal Court Remands —

(1) Circuit court or district court orders — When a federal court orders further action in a case before the Board, the parties are asked to provide a copy of the federal court order to the Board. Parties should not assume federal court orders are provided by the federal court to the Board.

(2) Copies of certified record — When a decision of the Board is reviewed by a federal court, the Board provides that court with a certified copy of the record before the Board. Copies of a certified record do not need to be included with submissions to the Board.

(3) Documents filed with federal court — Proceedings before a federal court are separate from proceedings before the Board. Documents submitted by parties to the federal court are not part of the record before the Board and may need to be submitted directly to the Board. However, parties should wait to submit such documents until the Board confirms that it has received the federal court's order. See Chapter 4.19 (Federal Court Remands). Also, parties must meet all other filing requirements covered in this chapter.

(g) Criminal Conviction Documents — Documents regarding criminal convictions must comport with the requirements set forth in 8 C.F.R. § 1003.41.

3.4   Filing Fees

(a) When Required — A filing fee must be submitted together with an appeal or motion filed directly with the Board in the following instances:

- any appeal filed with the Board (except an appeal of a custody bond determination)

- a motion to reopen (except a motion that is based exclusively on a claim for asylum)

- a motion to reconsider (except a motion that is based on an underlying claim for asylum)

See 8 C.F.R. §§ 1003.2(g)(2)(i), 1003.3, 1003.8. For purposes of determining filing fee requirements, the term "asylum" here includes withholding of removal, withholding of deportation, and claims under the Convention Against Torture and Other Cruel, Inhuman, or Degrading Treatment or Punishment.

If the appeal or motion is electronically filed through ECAS, the relevant fee, if any, must be paid electronically as well through the EOIR Payment Portal on EOIR's website. If the filing party is unable to pay the fee, they should request that the fee be waived. See subsection (c), below.

Filing fees should not be confused with *application* fees. See subsection (i), below.

(b) When Not Required — A filing fee is not required in the following instances:

- a custody bond appeal

- a motion to reopen that is based exclusively on a claim for asylum

- a motion to reconsider that is based on an underlying claim for asylum

- a motion filed while an appeal, a motion to reopen, or a motion to reconsider is already pending before the Board

- a motion requesting only a stay of removal, deportation, or exclusion

- a motion to recalendar

- any appeal or motion filed by DHS

- a motion that is agreed upon by all parties and is jointly filed (a "joint motion")

- an appeal or motion filed under a law, regulation, or directive that does not require a filing fee

See 8 C.F.R. §§ 1003.2(g)(2)(i) , 1003.3, 1003.8. For purposes of determining filing fee requirements, the term "asylum" here includes withholding of removal, withholding of deportation, and claims under the Convention Against Torture and Other Cruel, Inhuman, or Degrading Treatment or Punishment.

(c) When Waived — When an appeal or motion normally requires a filing fee, the Board has the discretion to waive that fee upon a showing of economic hardship or incapacity.

Fee waivers are *not* automatic but must be requested through the filing of a Fee Waiver Request (Form EOIR-26A). The Fee Waiver Request form must be filed along with the Notice of Appeal (Form EOIR-26) or the motion. The form requests information about monthly income and expenses and requires the applicant to declare, under penalty of perjury, that the applicant is unable to pay the fee due to personal economic hardship. If a fee waiver request does not establish the inability to pay the required fee, the requesting party will receive a rejection notice and the appeal or motion will be returned. However, the filer will be given 15-days to re-file the rejected appeal or motion with the fee or new fee waiver request, and any applicable filing deadline will be tolled during the 15-day cure period. See 8 C.F.R. § 1003.8(a)(3).

Fees are not reimbursed merely because the appeal is sustained, the motion is granted, or a party withdraws the appeal or motion.

(d) Amount of Payment — The filing fee, in all cases in which a fee is required except for a practitioner's appeal from a decision in disciplinary proceedings, is $110 and must be paid in the *precise* amount. If a fee is required, but is paid in any amount other than $110, except for an appeal in discipline proceedings, the filing will be rejected. See Chapter 3.1(c)(1) (Meaning of "rejected"). The filing fee for a Notice of Appeal from a Decision of an Adjudicating Official in a Practitioner Disciplinary Case (Form EOIR-45) is $675. The exact amount of $675 must be paid, any other amount other than $675, the filing will be rejected.

(e) Number of Payments for a Consolidated Proceeding — Only one fee should be paid in a consolidated proceeding. See Chapter 4.10(a) (Consolidated Appeals). For example, if family members appeared in consolidated proceeding before an immigration judge, they need file only one appeal and pay only one filing fee on appeal.

If the proceedings were not consolidated below by an immigration judge, a separate filing fee is required for each family member. For example, if spouses filed separate claims for relief and those claims were ruled upon separately by an immigration judge, their appeals would have to be filed separately, with a separate fee for each.

(f) Form of Payment — When a filing fee is required for an appeal or motion filed directly with the Board, the fee must be paid electronically, by check, or by money order in U.S. dollars. Checks or money orders must be drawn from a bank or institution that is located within the United States. 8 C.F.R. § 1003.8(a). Checks must be pre-printed with the name of the bank, as well as the account holder's name, address, and phone number. Checks and money orders are to be made payable to the "United States Department of Justice." The check or money order must include the full name and A-number of the respondent or, in the case of a consolidated proceeding, the lead respondent. Electronic payments must be submitted through the EOIR Payment Portal.

The Board does not accept cash. The Board uses the Treasury Department's OTCNet check capture process or Board fees can be paid electronically through ECAS. When you provide a check as payment, you authorize the Board either to use information from your check to make a one-time electronic fund transfer from your account or to process the payment as a check transaction. For inquiries, please contact the Clerk's Office by calling 703-605-1007. For information regarding the Privacy Act Statement, please see notice below:

Privacy Act – A Privacy Act Statement required by 5 U.S.C. § 552a(e)(3) stating our authority for soliciting and collecting the information from your check, and explaining the purposes and routine uses which will be made of your check information, is available from the Federal Register at: (https://www.federalregister.gov/articles/2003/02/04/03-2521/privacy-act-of-1974-as-amended-system-of-records), or by calling toll free at 1-866-945-7920 to obtain a copy by mail. Furnishing the check information is voluntary, but a decision not to do so may require you to make payment by money order.

(g) Defective or Missing Payment — If a filing fee is required for an appeal or motion but is not submitted or is defective, the filing will be rejected. See Chapter 3.1(c)(1) (Meaning of "rejected"). If a fee payment is not in the correct amount of $110, except for an appeal in discipline proceedings, the filing will be rejected. The filing fee for a Notice of Appeal from a Decision of an Adjudicating Official in a Practitioner

Disciplinary Case (Form EOIR-45) is $675. If the fee payment is not in the correct amount of $675, the filing will be rejected. If a fee payment is uncollectible (for example, a check "bounces"), the appeal or motion will be dismissed or denied as improperly filed.

(h) Attaching the Fee — For appeals paper-filed with the Board, any filing fee payment should be stapled to the Notice of Appeal (Form EOIR-26 or Form EOIR-45) as indicated on the form. For motions, any fee payment should be stapled to the cover sheet. For any fee payment made electronically, the fee receipt should be submitted with the filing.

(i) Application Fees — The Board does not collect fees for underlying applications for relief (e.g., adjustment of status, cancellation of removal). Application fees should be paid to DHS or other agency in accordance with the instructions on the application form.

When a motion before the Board is based upon newly available eligibility for relief, payment of the fee for the underlying application is not a prerequisite to filing the motion. Jurisdiction over an application for new relief lies with the immigration courts, and thus the application fee need not be paid unless and until the application comes before an immigration judge.

3.5   Briefs

The requirements for briefs are discussed elsewhere in this manual. See Chapters 4.6 (Appeal Briefs), 5.4 (Motion Briefs).

3.6   Expedite Requests

Parties seeking urgent Board action should follow the procedures set forth in Chapter 6 (Stays and Expedite Requests).

Chapter 4 Appeals of Immigration Judge Decisions

4.1   Types of Appeals

The Board entertains appeals from the decisions of immigration judges and certain decisions of the Department of Homeland Security (DHS). See Chapter 1.4(a) (Jurisdiction). Unless otherwise indicated, this chapter is limited to appeals from the decisions of immigration judges pertaining to the removal, deportation, or exclusion of noncitizens.

Other kinds of appeals are discussed in the following chapters:

Chapter 7   Bond

Chapter 9   Visa Petitions

Chapter 10   Fines

Chapter 11   Discipline

4.2   Process

(a) Immigration Judge Decision — An immigration judge presides over courtroom proceedings in removal, deportation, exclusion, and other proceedings. See Chapter 1.2(c) (Relationship to the Immigration Court). The parties in such proceedings are the respondents and DHS. See Chapter 1.2(d) (Relationship to the Department of Homeland Security (DHS)).

(1) Oral vs. written — The decision of an immigration judge may be rendered either orally or in writing. When a decision is rendered orally, the immigration judge recites the entire decision in the parties' presence and provides them with a written memorandum order summarizing the oral decision. When a decision is rendered in writing, the decision is served on the parties by first class mail or by personal service, mail, or electronic notification. See 8 C.F.R § 1003.37.

(2) Appeal to the Board vs. motion before the immigration judge — After the immigration judge renders a final decision, a party may either file an appeal with the Board or file a motion with the immigration judge. See Chapter 4.14 (Interlocutory Appeals). Once a party files an appeal with the Board, jurisdiction is vested with the Board, and the immigration judge is divested of jurisdiction over the case. Accordingly, once an appeal has been filed with the Board, an immigration judge may no longer entertain a motion to reopen or a motion to reconsider. For that reason, if a party first files a motion with the immigration judge and then files an appeal with the Board, the immigration judge loses jurisdiction over the motion, and the record of proceedings is transferred to the Board for consideration of the appeal.

(3) Certification vs. appeal — Certification to the Board is entirely separate and distinct from the filing of an appeal, and the two should not be confused. See Chapter 4.18 (Certification by an Immigration Judge).

(b) Filing — If an appeal is taken from the decision of an immigration judge, it must be filed properly and within the time allowed. See Chapters 3 (Filing with the Board), 4.5 (Appeal Deadlines). An appeal of an immigration judge decision must be filed directly with the Board, using the Notice of Appeal (Form EOIR-26). 8 C.F.R. § 1003.3(a). See Chapter 3.1 (Delivery and Receipt). The appeal may *not* be filed with DHS or an immigration court. Erroneous filing of an appeal with DHS or an immigration court does not constitute filing with the Board and will not excuse the filing party from the appeal deadline.

If an appeal is received by the Board but has not been properly filed (for example, the filing fee is missing or Proof of Service has not been completed), the appeal may be rejected. See Chapter 3.1(c) (Defective Filings); Chapter 3.1(c)(1) (Meaning of "rejected"). Rejection does *not* extend the filing deadline, except in cases of a denied fee waiver, as explained in Chapter 3.4(c) (When Waived). Instead, it can result in an untimely filing and, ultimately, dismissal of the appeal. See Chapter 4.5(b) (Extensions).

(c) Stays — A respondent may seek a stay of deportation or stay of removal while an appeal is pending before the Board. Stays are automatic in some instances, but discretionary in others. Stays are discussed in Chapter 6 (Stays and Expedite Requests).

(d) Processing — Once an appeal is properly filed, a written receipt is sent to both the respondent and DHS. The Board will then obtain the record of proceedings from the immigration court. In appropriate cases, a briefing schedule is provided to both sides. Also, in appropriate cases, a transcript is prepared, and copies are sent to the parties along with the briefing schedule. See subsections (e), (f) below.

(e) Briefing Schedule — When a Notice of Appeal is filed, a receipt is issued to acknowledge receipt of the appeal. A briefing schedule is then issued in which the parties are notified of the deadlines for filing a brief. See Chapter 4.7 (Briefing Deadlines). The briefs must arrive at the Board by the dates set in the briefing schedule. See Chapter 3.1 (Delivery and Receipt). In the event that a briefing extension is requested and granted, a briefing extension notice is issued. See Chapter 4.7(c) (Extensions).

For federal court remands, the Board determines whether a brief is required. If a briefing schedule is set, the parties are notified of the deadlines for filing, and the briefs must arrive at the Board by the set dates. See Chapters 3.1 (Delivery and Receipt), 4.7 (Briefing Deadlines).

(f) Transcription — The Board transcribes immigration court proceedings in appropriate cases.

(1) Preparation of transcripts — The Board transcribes proceedings, where appropriate, after receiving a properly filed appeal from the decision of an immigration judge. Where a transcript is prepared, the transcript is sent to both parties along with the briefing schedule via regular mail, or through ECAS in eligible cases. The Board does not entertain requests to send transcripts by overnight delivery or other means.

(2) Requests for transcripts — Transcripts are not normally prepared for the following types of appeals: bond determinations; denials of motions to reopen (including motions to reopen in absentia proceedings); denials of motions to reconsider; and interlocutory appeals.

Proceedings of these types may in some instances be transcribed at the discretion of the Board. If a party desires a transcript for any of these types of proceedings, the party should send correspondence with a cover page labeled "REQUEST FOR TRANSCRIPTION." See Appendix E (Cover Pages). That correspondence should briefly state the reasons for the request. However, a request for transcription does *not* affect the briefing schedule. Parties are still required to meet briefing deadlines.

Copies of digital audio or cassette tape recordings of hearings may be requested by the parties and their practitioner of record. A Freedom of Information Act (FOIA) request is not required. Parties may obtain a copy that is not prohibited (e.g., classified information, subject to protective order). Requests for copies may be made to the Board in person, by mail, or by email. The Board encourages parties to request a copy of the digitally- or cassette tape-recorded hearings by email using "EOIR.BIA.ROP.Requests@udoj.gov." This email address is only to be used for requests for a copy of the official record or portion of the official record. The Board does not provide self-service copying. Alternatively, the parties may file a request pursuant to FOIA. See Chapter 13 (Requesting Records).

For more information on digitally- or cassette-recorded hearings, parties should consult the Immigration Court Practice Manual, which is available on the EOIR website.

(3) Defects in the transcript — Obvious defects in the transcript (e.g., photocopying errors, large gaps in the recorded record) should be brought to the immediate attention of the Clerk's Office. Such requests should be filed separately under a cover page titled "REQUEST FOR CORRECTION OF TRANSCRIPT." See Appendix A (Directory), Appendix E (Cover Pages). The Board, in its discretion, may remedy the defect where appropriate and feasible.

Defects do *not* excuse the parties from existing briefing deadlines. Those deadlines remain in effect until the parties are notified otherwise. See Chapter 4.7(c) (Extensions).

Where the Board does not or cannot remedy the purported defect in the transcript, and the party believes that defect to be significant to the party's argument or the adjudication of the appeal, the party should identify the defect and argue its significance with specificity in the appeal brief. The Board recommends that the brief be supported by a sworn, detailed statement. The

Board will consider any allegations of transcript error in the course of adjudicating the appeal.

(4) Corrected oral decisions — When an immigration judge issues an oral decision, the immigration judge reviews the transcription of the oral decision and may make minor, clerical corrections to the decision. These corrected decisions are returned to the Board and served on the parties. If a party believes the corrections are significant to the party's argument or the adjudication of the appeal, the party should identify the correction and its significance with specificity in the appeal brief. Corrections do *not* excuse the parties from existing briefing deadlines. If the corrected decision is served after the briefing schedule has expired, the parties should file a "Motion to Accept Supplemental Brief."
See Chapter 4.6(g) (Supplemental Briefs).

(5) Stipulated record of proceedings — Whether or not a transcript is available, the respondent and DHS may prepare and sign a stipulation regarding the facts of events that transpired below. The parties may also correct errors or omissions in the record by stipulation.

(g) Oral Argument — The Board occasionally grants oral argument at the request of one of the parties. In such cases, parties present their case orally to a panel of three or more Board Members in a courtroom setting. See Chapter 8 (Oral Argument).

(h) Record on Appeal — The actual contents of the record on appeal vary from case to case, but generally include the following items: charging documents; hearing notices; notices of appearance; applications for relief and any accompanying documents; court-filed papers and exhibits; transcript of proceedings and oral decision of the immigration judge, if prepared; written memorandum order or decision of the immigration judge; Notice of Appeal; briefing schedules; briefs; motions; correspondence; and any prior decisions by the Board. Note that the Board does not automatically provide a copy of the record of proceedings (ROP) to the parties to the proceedings upon filing an appeal. Parties may receive a copy of the ROP if they file a separate request for a copy. See Chapter 1.5(e)(3) (Copies for parties).

(i) Decision — Upon entry of a decision, the Board serves its decision upon the parties. See Chapter 1.4(d) (Board Decisions). The decision is sent by regular mail to the parties, and/or through ECAS in eligible cases. A courtesy copy of the decision is also sent by regular mail to a represented respondent.

4.3   Parties

(a) Parties to an Appeal —

(1) The respondent — Only a respondent who was the subject of an immigration court proceeding, or the respondent's practitioner of record, may file a Notice of Appeal (Form EOIR-26). An unrepresented or pro se respondent may receive assistance with the Form EOIR-26 from a practitioner who drafted, completed, or prepared the Form EOIR-26 pursuant to a limited appearance for document assistance. See Chapter 2.1(c) (Limited Appearance for Document Assistance); 3.3(b) (Signatures).

The Form EOIR-26 must identify the names and A-numbers of every person included in the appeal. *The appeal is limited to those persons identified.* 8 C.F.R. § 1003.3(a)(1). Thus, families should take special care – in each and every filing – to identify by name and A-number every family member included in the appeal. See Chapters 4.4(b)(3) (How many to file), 4.10 (Combining and Separating Appeals).

(2) DHS — DHS is deemed a party to the immigration court proceeding. See Chapter 1.2(d) (Relationship to the Department of Homeland Security (DHS)). Thus, DHS is entitled to appeal an immigration judge decision and is deemed a party for any appeal filed by the respondent. An appeal filed by DHS must also identify the names and A-numbers of every person from whose proceeding DHS is filing that appeal.

(3) Other persons or entities — No other person or entity may file an appeal of an immigration judge decision.

(b) Parties who have Waived Appeal —

(1) Effect of appeal waiver — If the opportunity to appeal is knowingly and intelligently waived, the decision of the immigration judge becomes final. See 8 C.F.R. § 1003.39. If a party waives appeal at the conclusion of proceedings before the immigration judge, that party generally may not file an appeal thereafter. See 8 C.F.R. § 1003.3(a)(1); *Matter of Shih*, 20 I&N Dec. 697 (BIA 1993). See also 8 C.F.R. § 1003.1(d)(2)(i)(G).

(2) Challenging a waiver of appeal — Generally, a party who waives appeal cannot retract, withdraw, or otherwise undo that waiver. If a party wishes to challenge the validity of their waiver of appeal, the party may do so in one of two ways: either in a timely motion filed with the immigration judge that explains why the appeal waiver was not valid, or in an appeal filed directly with the Board that explains why the appeal waiver was not valid. *Matter of Patino*, 23 I&N Dec. 74 (BIA 2001). Once an appeal is filed, jurisdiction vests with the Board, and the motion can no longer be ruled upon by the immigration judge. See Chapter 4.2(a)(2) (Appeal to the Board vs. motion before the immigration judge).

(c) Representation — A party to an appeal may appear without representation ("pro se") or with representation. See Chapter 2 (Appearances before the Board). If a party wishes to be represented, they may be represented by a practitioner of record. See 8 C.F.R. § 1292.1; Chapter 2.1(b) (Entering an Appearance as the Practitioner of Record). Whenever a party is represented, the party should submit all filings, documents, and communications to the Board through their practitioner of record. See Chapter 2.1(b)(7) (Filings After Entry of Appearance as Practitioner of Record). An unrepresented or pro se party may receive assistance from a practitioner with the drafting, completion, or filling in of blank spaces of a specific appeal, motion, brief, form, or other document or set of documents intended to be filed with the Board pursuant to a limited appearance for document assistance. See Chapter 2.1(c) (Limited Appearance for Document Assistance).

(d) Persons not Party to the Appeal — Only a party to an appeal, or a party's practitioner of record, may file an appeal, motion, or document or send correspondence regarding that appeal. An unrepresented or pro se party may receive assistance from a practitioner with the drafting, completion, or filling in of blank spaces of a specific appeal, motion, brief, form, or other document or set of documents intended to be filed with the Board pursuant to a limited appearance for document assistance. See Chapter 2.1(c) (Limited Appearance for Document Assistance); 3.3(b) (Signatures). Family members, employers, and other third parties may not submit appeals, filings, or supporting documents and material. Filings received from third parties will be returned to the sender where possible.

If anyone who is not a party to the appeal wishes to make a submission to the Board regarding a particular case, that person or entity should make the submission through one of the parties. Third parties who wish to appear as amicus curiae should consult Chapter 2.10 (Amicus Curiae).

4.4   Filing an Appeal

(a) Rules for Filing — An appeal must be filed in accordance with the general rules for filing. See Chapter 3.1 (Delivery and Receipt). For the order in which documents should be filed, see Chapter 3.3(c)(1)(A) (Appeals).

(b) Notice of Appeal — For any appeal of an immigration judge decision, a completed and executed Notice of Appeal (Form EOIR-26) must be timely filed with the Board. See Chapter 4.5 (Appeal Deadlines). See also 8 C.F.R. § 1003.3(a)(1). Parties must read carefully and comply with the instructions on the Notice of Appeal (Form EOIR-26).

(1) When to file — See Chapter 4.5 (Appeal Deadlines).

(2) Where to file — For appeals of immigration judge decisions, the Notice of Appeal (Form EOIR-26) must be filed with the Board. It may *not* be filed with DHS or an immigration court. Filing an appeal of an immigration judge decision with DHS or an immigration court will not be accepted as proper filing with the Board. See Chapter 1.6(d) (Mail and other forms of delivery).

(3) How many to file — A single Notice of Appeal (Form EOIR-26) must be filed for each respondent who is appealing the decision of an immigration judge, *unless* the appeal is from proceedings that were consolidated by the immigration judge. See Chapters 4.3(a) (Parties to an Appeal), 4.10(a) (Consolidated Appeals). Only the original Notice of Appeal must be filed. Additional copies of the Notice of Appeal need not be submitted.

(4) Completing the Notice of Appeal — For appeals of immigration judge decisions, the Notice of Appeal (Form EOIR-26) contains instructions on how to complete the form. Parties should be careful to complete the form accurately and completely.

(A) A-numbers — The A-number of *every* person included in the appeal should appear on the form.

(B) Important data — The party appealing should make sure the form is completed in full, including the parts of the form that request the date of the immigration judge's oral decision or written order, and the type of proceeding (removal, deportation, exclusion, asylum, bond, denial of a motion to reopen by an immigration judge, or denial of a motion to reconsider by an immigration judge).

(C) Brief in support of the appeal — The appealing party must indicate on the Notice of Appeal (Form EOIR-26) whether or not a brief will be filed in support of the appeal. If a party indicates that a brief will be filed and thereafter fails to file a brief, the appeal may be summarily dismissed. See Chapters 4.7(e) (Decision not to File a Brief), 4.16 (Summary Dismissal). The Board strongly encourages the filing of briefs. See Chapter 4.6 (Appeal Briefs).

(D) Grounds for the appeal — Space is provided on the Notice of Appeal for a concise statement to identify the grounds for the appeal. The statement of appeal is not limited to the space on the form but may be continued on additional sheets of paper. Any additional sheets, however, should be attached to the Notice of Appeal (Form EOIR-26) and labeled with the name and A-number of everyone included in the appeal.

Parties are advised that vague generalities, generic recitations of the law, and general assertions of immigration judge error are unlikely to apprise the Board of the reasons for appeal.

(E) Summary dismissal — If neither the Notice of Appeal (Form EOIR-26) nor the documents filed with it adequately identify the basis for the appeal, the appeal may be summarily dismissed. See Chapter 4.16(b) (Failure to Specify Grounds for Appeal). If a party indicates on the Notice of Appeal that a brief will be filed in support of the appeal and thereafter fails to file a brief, the appeal may be summarily dismissed. See Chapter 4.7(e) (Decision not to File a Brief). There are other grounds for summary dismissal. See 8 C.F.R. § 1003.1(d)(2). See also Chapter 4.16 (Summary Dismissal).

(5) Mistakes to avoid —

(A) Mixing unrelated appeals — Parties and practitioners should not "mix" unrelated appeals on one Notice of Appeal (Form EOIR-26). Each immigration judge decision must be appealed separately. For example, one Notice of Appeal should not combine the appeal of a bond determination and the appeal of an immigration judge decision regarding eligibility for relief. See Chapter 7.3(a)(1) (Separate Notice of Appeal). The appealing party should attach a copy of the decision being appealed to the Notice of Appeal.

(B) Using the Notice of Appeal for motions — A Notice of Appeal (Form EOIR-26) may *not* be used to file a motion with the Board. See Chapter 5 (Motions before the Board).

(C) Using the Notice of Appeal to appeal to a federal court — A Notice of Appeal (Form EOIR-26) may not be used to challenge a decision *made by* the Board. In this instance, the proper filing is a motion to reconsider with the Board or an action in the appropriate United States district or circuit court.

(c) Proof of Service — The Certificate of Service portion of the Notice of Appeal (Form EOIR-26) must be completed. See Chapter 3.2(d) (Proof of Service).

(d) Fee or Fee Waiver — The appeal must be accompanied by the appropriate filing fee, fee receipt, or a completed Fee Waiver Request (Form EOIR-26A). 8 C.F.R. §§ 1003.3(a)(1), 1003.8. See Chapter 3.4 (Filing Fees).

(e) Notice of Appearance — If a party is represented by a practitioner of record or has received assistance from a practitioner with the drafting, completion, or filling in of blank spaces of a Notice of Appeal (Form EOIR-26), a Notice of Appearance (Form EOIR-27) or Notice of Limited Appearance (Form EOIR-60), respectively, must accompany the Notice of Appeal. See Chapter 2.1 (Representation and Appearances Generally), 3.3(b) (Signatures), 4.3(c) (Representation).

(f) Copy of Order — Parties are encouraged to include a copy of either the memorandum order of the oral decision or the written decision being appealed.

(g) Confirmation of Receipt — The Board routinely issues receipts for Notices of Appeal (Form EOIR-26). The Board does not provide receipts for appellate briefs or supplemental filings, aside from any ECAS filing notifications. See Chapter 3.1(d) (Filing Receipts).

4.5   Appeal Deadlines

(a) Due Date — A Notice of Appeal (Form EOIR-26) must be filed no later than 30 calendar days after the immigration judge renders an oral decision or mails or provides electronic notification of a written decision. 8 C.F.R. § 1003.38(b).

The 30-day period is computed as described in Chapter 3.1(b)(2) (Computation of time). The Board does not follow the "mailbox rule" but calculates deadlines according to the time of receipt at the Clerk's Office. See Chapter 3.1 (Delivery and Receipt). The 30-day deadline and method of computation applies to all parties, including persons detained by DHS or other federal or state authorities.

(b) Extensions — The regulations set strict deadlines for the filing of an appeal, and the Board's authority to extend or toll the time in which to file a Notice of Appeal (Form EOIR-26) is limited, as described below. See 8 C.F.R § 1003.38(b).

(1) ECAS system outages (electronic filing) — System outages may occur that make electronic filing through ECAS unavailable and may impact filing deadlines for a case where electronic filing is mandatory. If EOIR determines that an unplanned outage has occurred, filing deadlines that occur on the last day for filing in a specific case will be extended until the first day of system availability that is not a Saturday, Sunday, or legal holiday. See 8 C.F.R. § 1003.3(g)(2). Note that planned system outages will not impact filing deadlines since these can be proactively addressed by the parties. EOIR will maintain an ECAS Outage Log that will note planned and unplanned ECAS system outages.

(2) Fee waiver denied — If a Fee Waiver Request (Form EOIR-26A) does not establish the inability to pay the required fee, the requesting party will receive a rejection notice and the appeal will be returned. However, the filer will be given 15 days to re-file the rejected appeal with the fee or new fee waiver request, and the applicable appeal filing deadline will be tolled during the 15-day cure period. See 8 C.F.R. § 1003.8(a)(3). See Chapter 3.4(c) (When Waived).

(3) Equitable tolling — The Board has determined that the principles of equitable tolling apply as an exception to the 30-day regulatory deadline for filing an appeal as provided by 8 C.F.R. § 1003.38. See *Matter of Morales-Morales*, 28 I&N Dec. 714 (BIA 2023). The party seeking equitable tolling must show both diligence in the filing of the Notice of Appeal and that an extraordinary circumstance prevented the timely filing. *Id.*

If a party wishes the Board to consider this equitable tolling exception to the filing deadline, the Notice of Appeal (Form EOIR-26) must be accompanied by a written motion entitled "MOTION TO ACCEPT LATE APPEAL" and comply generally with the rules and procedures for filings. See Chapter 3 (Filing with the Board), Chapter 4(b) (Filing). A motion to accept an untimely appeal must clearly establish both diligence in the filing of the notice of appeal and that an extraordinary circumstance prevented the filing. The motion should be supported by affidavits, declarations, and other evidence. The Board will advise the parties of its decision on the motion.

(c) Detained Persons — Detained persons are subject to the same 30-day appeal deadline. All appeals, regardless of origin, must be received by the Board in the time allotted. An appeal is not timely filed simply because it is deposited in the detention facility's internal mail system or is given to facility staff to mail prior to the deadline.

4.6   Appeal Briefs

(a) Filing — An appeal brief must comply with the general requirements for filing. See Chapter 3.1 (Delivery and Receipt). The appeal brief must be timely. See Chapter 4.7 (Briefing Deadlines). It should have a cover page. See Appendix E (Cover Pages). The briefing notice from the Board should be stapled on top of the cover page or otherwise attached to the brief in accordance with the instructions on the briefing notice. The brief must be served on the other party. See Chapter 3.2(d) (Proof of Service). There is no fee for filing a brief.

(1) Appeals from immigration judge decisions — For appeals from immigration judge decisions, the appeal brief must be filed directly with the Board. 8 C.F.R § 1003.3(c)(1).

(2) Appeals from Department of Homeland Security decisions — For appeals from decisions of the Department of Homeland Security (DHS), the brief should be filed with DHS, not the Board, and in accordance with the instructions on the appeal form.

(b) Brief-Writing Guidelines — A brief advises the Board of a party's position and arguments. A well-written brief is in any party's best interest and is therefore of great importance to the Board. The brief should be clear, concise, well-organized, and should cite the record and legal authorities fully, fairly, and accurately.

Briefs should always recite those facts which are appropriate and germane to the adjudication of the appeal, and should cite proper legal authority, where such authority is available. See Chapter 4.6(d) (Citation). Briefs should not belabor facts or law that are not in dispute. Parties are encouraged to expressly identify in their briefs when they agree with the immigration judge's recitation of facts or law.

Briefs should *always* be paginated. Parties must limit the body of their briefs to 50 pages unless otherwise directed by the Board. In computing the length limit, headings, footnotes, and quotations count toward the limit. In addition, regardless of the descriptive heading, the page count toward the page limit includes any statement of facts and procedural history, statement of issues presented for review, standard of review, summary of the argument, argument, and conclusion. By contrast, the following items do not count toward the page limit:

- cover page;

- table of contents;

- table of citations;

- signature block;

- certificate / proof of service;

- addendum containing statutes, rules, regulations, or case law; and

- supporting documentation.

Oversized briefs unnecessarily burden the Board. Motions to accept briefs that exceed the page limitation established by the Board are disfavored and will not be granted absent a showing of extraordinary and compelling circumstances. If a party files an oversized brief, the brief should be accompanied with a written motion entitled "MOTION TO EXTEND PAGE LIMIT" that generally complies with the rules and procedures for motions and filings. See Chapter 3 (Filing with the Board), Chapter 5.2 (Filing a Motion). Thus, the motion and brief need to be submitted together. If an oversized brief is filed without a motion to extend the page limit, the brief will be rejected.

Motions to extend the page limit also should include a statement of reasons for exceeding the page limitation that demonstrates extraordinary and compelling reasons. Note that stating that a case involves asylum law or complex legal issues is not sufficient. If the motion is granted, the motion and brief are incorporated into the record, and the brief is considered by the Board. If the motion is denied, the motion is retained as part of the record, but the brief is removed without consideration. In either case, the parties are notified of the Board's decision. Motions to reconsider denials will not be considered.

(c) Format — Briefs should comport with the requirements set out in Chapter 3.3 (Documents).

(1) Signature — Briefs should be signed by the person who prepared or drafted the brief. See Chapter 3.3(b) (Signatures). If prepared or drafted by a registered attorney or accredited representative, the EOIR ID number should also be provided. See Chapter 2.1(a) (Right to Counsel and Individuals Authorized to Provide Representation and Make Appearances), Chapter 3.3(b) (Signatures).

(2) A-number — The A-number of each respondent should appear on the cover page of the brief and on the bottom right corner of each page thereafter.

If a respondent has more than one A-number assigned to them, then every A-number should appear on the cover page of the brief.

If a brief is filed in a consolidated appeal and a comprehensive listing of A-numbers is impractical on every page, the first page of the brief should contain the name and A-number of every respondent included in the appeal. The A-number of the lead respondent followed by "et al.", should appear as a footer on the bottom right corner of each page thereafter. See Chapter 4.10(a) (Consolidated Appeals).

Unrelated proceedings should not be addressed in the same brief, *unless* proceedings have been consolidated by the immigration judge or the Board. If proceedings have been consolidated, this should be stated in the introductory portion of the brief. If proceedings have not been consolidated, a separate brief should be filed for each individual case. If a party wishes unrelated appeals to be considered together (but not consolidated), this may be requested in the introductory portion of the brief. See Chapter 4.10 (Combining and Separating Appeals).

(3) Caption — Parties should use captions and cover pages in all filings. See Chapter 3.3(c)(6) (Cover page and caption), Appendix E (Cover Pages).

(4) Recommended contents — The following items should be included in the brief:

- a concise statement of facts and procedural history relevant to issues presented in the case

- a statement of issues presented for review

- the standard of review

- succinct, clear, and accurate summary of the argument

- the argument

- a short conclusion stating the precise relief or remedy sought

(5) References to parties — To avoid confusion, use of "appellant" and "appellee" is discouraged. When litigation titles are desired or necessary, the following guidelines should be followed:

- removal proceedings: the noncitizen is referred to as "respondent"

- deportation proceedings: the noncitizen is referred to as "respondent"

- exclusion proceedings: the noncitizen is referred to as "applicant"

- asylum-only proceedings: the noncitizen is referred to as "applicant"

- withholding-only proceedings: the noncitizen is referred to as "applicant"

- bond proceedings: the noncitizen is referred to as "respondent"

- visa petition proceedings: the sponsoring individual or entity is referred to as "petitioner" and the noncitizen being petitioned for is referred to as "beneficiary"

- all proceedings: the immigration judge should be referred to as "the immigration judge"

- all proceedings: the Department of Homeland Security should be referred to as "DHS" or "Department of Homeland Security"

Care must be taken not to confuse DHS with the immigration court or the immigration judge. See Chapter 1.4(f) (Department of Homeland Security).

Complete names, titles, agency designations, or descriptive terms are preferred when referring to third parties.

(6) Statement of facts — A brief's statement of facts should be concise. If facts are not in dispute, the brief should simply and expressly adopt the facts as set forth in the decision of the immigration judge. If facts are in dispute or, in the party's estimation, are insufficiently developed in the decision of the immigration judge, the party's brief should concisely set out the facts clearly and expressly identify the points of contention.

Facts, like case law, require citations. Parties should support factual assertions by citation to the record. When referring to the record, parties should follow Chapter 4.6(d) (Citation). Sweeping assertions of fact that are made without citation to their location in the record are not helpful. Likewise, facts that were not established on the record may not be introduced for the first time on appeal. *Matter of Fedorenko*, 19 I&N Dec. 57 (BIA 1984).

The Board admonishes all parties: Do not misstate or misrepresent the facts, or omit unfavorable facts that are relevant to the adjudication of the appeal. A brief's accuracy and integrity are paramount to the persuasiveness of the argument and the proper adjudication of the appeal.

(7) Footnotes — Substantive arguments should be restricted to the text of the brief. Excessive use of footnotes is discouraged.

(8) Headings and other markers — The brief should employ headings, subheadings, and spacing to make the brief more readable. Short paragraphs with topic sentences and proper headings facilitate the coherence and cohesion of an argument.

(9) Chronologies — A brief should contain a chronology of the facts, especially in those instances where the facts are complicated or involve several events. Charts or similar graphic representations that chronicle events are welcome.

(10) Multiple briefs — The Board prefers that arguments in an appeal brief not incorporate by cross-reference arguments that have been made elsewhere, such as in a prehearing brief or motion brief. Whenever possible, arguments should be contained in full in the appeal brief.

(d) Citation — Parties are expected to provide complete and clear citation to all authorities, factual or legal. The Board asks all parties to comply with the citation conventions articulated here and in Appendix I (Citations).

(1) Board decisions (precedent) — In the past, the Board issued precedent decisions in slip opinion or "Interim Decision" form. See Chapter 1.4(d)(1)(C) (Interim Decisions). Citations to the Interim Decisions form are now greatly disfavored.

Precedent Board decisions are published in an "I&N Dec." form. See Chapter 1.4(d) (Board Decisions). Citations to Board decisions should be made in accordance with their publication in *Administrative Decisions Under Immigration & Nationality Laws of the United States*. The proper citation form includes the volume number, the reporter abbreviation ("I&N Dec."), the first page of the decision, the name of the adjudicator (BIA, A.G., etc.), and the year of the decision. Example: *Matter of Gomez-Giraldo*, 20 I&N Dec. 957 (BIA 1995).

All precedent decisions should be cited as "Matter of." The use of "*In re*" is not favored. Example: *Matter of Yanez*, 23 I&N Dec. 390 (BIA 2002), not *In re Yanez*, 23 I&N Dec. 390 (BIA 2002).

Citations to a specific point in a precedent decision should include the precise page number(s) on which the point appears. Example: *Matter of Artigas*, 23 I&N Dec. 99, 100 (BIA 2001).

Citations to a separate opinion in a precedent decision should include a parenthetical identifying whether it is a dissent or concurrence. Example: *Matter of Artigas*, 23 I&N Dec. 99, 109-110 (BIA 2001) (dissent).

(2) Board decisions (non-precedent) — Citation to non-precedent Board cases by parties not bound by the decision is discouraged. When it is necessary to refer to an unpublished decision, the citation should include the initials of the respondent's full name separated by hyphens, the A-number with all but the last three digits of the number replaced with X's, and a parenthetical containing the abbreviation "BIA" as the adjudicating body, as well as an abbreviation of the month as part of the precise date of the decision. Because the Board uses "*Matter of*" as a signal for a published or precedent case, do not use "*Matter of.*"

- For example: John Jonathan Smith, A123-456-789, BIA 12/20/2020 would become J-J-S-, AXXX-XXX-789 (BIA Dec. 20, 2020).

Where an unpublished Board decision is obtained from EOIR's FOIA Reading Room, the citation should be placed within a parenthetical containing the assigned Folder Name (also known as Title or File number assigned to Download Folder), the abbreviation "BIA" as the adjudicating body, and an abbreviation of the month as part of the precise date of the decision. As noted above, because the Board uses "*Matter of*" of as a signal for published or precedent case, do not use "*Matter of.*"

- For example: Folder Name 1234567, Decision Date 10/2/2023 would become (1234567, BIA Oct. 2, 2023).

Further, when a Board unpublished decision is cited, a copy of the decision should be provided whenever possible. See Chapter 1.4(d)(2) (Unpublished decisions).

(3) Attorney General (precedent) — When the Attorney General issues a precedent decision, the decision is published in the *Administrative Decisions Under Immigration & Nationality Laws of the United States*. Attorney General precedent decisions should be cited in accordance with the same rules set forth in subsections (1) and (2), above.

(4) Department of Homeland Security (precedent) — Certain precedent decisions of the Department of Homeland Security, as well as those of the former Immigration and Naturalization Service, appear in the *Administrative Decisions Under Immigration & Nationality Laws of the United States*. These decisions should be cited in accordance with the same rules set forth in subsections (1) and (2), above.

(5) Federal and state court cases — Federal and state court decisions should be cited according to standard legal convention, as identified by the latest edition of *A Uniform System of Citation*, commonly known as the "Bluebook." If the case being cited is unpublished, a copy of that case should be provided.

(6) Statutes, rules, regulations, and other legal authorities and sources — Statutes, rules, regulations, and other standard sources of law should be cited according to standard legal convention, as identified by the latest edition of *A Uniform System of Citation*, commonly known as the "Bluebook." Sources of law or information that are peculiar to immigration law (e.g., the Foreign Affairs Manual) should be cited according to the convention of the immigration bar or cited in such a way as to make the source clear and accessible to the reader. Where citation is made to a source that is not readily available to the Board or the other party, a copy should be attached to the brief. See Chapter 3.3(e) (Source Materials).

(7) Transcript of proceedings — If an argument on appeal is based on an error in fact, procedure, or conduct that is manifested in the transcript, the Notice of Appeal or brief should provide citations to the transcript. Passages in the transcript of proceedings should be cited according to page number: "Tr. at _____." Line citations are welcome, but not necessary.

Where a transcript is not prepared, the audio recording should be cited as "Hearing for" and include the respondent's name, the A-number, and the date and time of the hearing. Example: "Hearing for John Smith, A012 345 679, February 11, 2014, at 1:00 p.m." If a party obtains a compact disk ("CD") of a hearing that was digitally recorded, the numbered tracks of the CD should not be cited. Rather, the relevant portion of the recording should be quoted in the citing party's brief, identifying what portion of the hearing the quotation took place (e.g., direct examination, cross-examination). See Chapter 4.2(f) (Transcription).

(8) Decision of the immigration judge — If an argument on appeal is based on an error in the immigration judge's decision, the decision of the immigration judge, whether rendered orally or in writing, should be cited as "I.J. at _____." If the reference is to a decision other than the decision being appealed, the citation should indicate the nature of the proceeding and the date. Example: "I.J. bond decision at 5 (Jan. 3, 2023)."

(9) Text from briefs — Text from the respondent's brief should be cited as "Applicant's brief at _____" or "Respondent's brief at _____", whichever is appropriate. Text from the DHS brief should be cited as "DHS brief at _____."

(10) Exhibits — Exhibits designated during the hearing should be cited as they were designated by the immigration judge. Example: "Exh. _____." Exhibits accompanying an appeal, brief, or motion should identify the exhibit and what it is attached to. Example: "Motion to Reopen Exh. 2."

(11) Certified record — When a decision of the Board is reviewed by a federal court, the Board provides that court with a certified copy of the record before the Board. See Chapter 1.4(h) (Federal Courts). The Board does not cite to the certified record in subsequent proceedings, and neither should the parties. Parties should instead follow the citation conventions discussed in the subsections above.

(e) Consolidated Briefs — Where cases have been consolidated, one brief may be submitted on behalf of all the respondents in the consolidated proceeding, provided that every respondent's full name and A-number appear on the consolidated brief. See generally Chapters 4.6(c)(2) (A-number), 4.10(a) (Consolidated appeals). A consolidated brief may not be filed if the cases have not been consolidated by the Board or an immigration judge.

(f) Response Briefs — When the appealing party files an appeal brief, the other party may file a "response brief," in accordance with the briefing schedule issued by the Board. See Chapter 4.7 (Briefing Deadlines).

If the appealing party fails to file a brief, the other party may nonetheless file one, provided it is filed in accordance with the briefing schedule issued by the Board.

(g) Supplemental Briefs — The Board usually does not accept supplemental briefs filed outside the period granted in the briefing schedule, except as described below.

(1) New authorities — Whenever a party discovers new authority subsequent to filing of a brief in a particular case, the party should notify the Board of the new authority through correspondence with a cover page entitled "STATEMENT OF NEW LEGAL AUTHORITIES." See Appendix E (Cover Pages). Such correspondence must be served upon the other party. See Chapter 3.2 (Service). It must also be limited to the citation of new authorities and may not contain any legal argument or discussion. Parties are admonished that the Board will not consider any correspondence that appears in form or substance to be a supplemental brief.

(2) New argument — If a party discovers new authority and wishes to file a supplemental brief, or in any way substitute for the original brief, the party should submit the brief along with a "MOTION TO ACCEPT SUPPLEMENTAL BRIEF" that complies generally with the rules for motions, including service on the opposing party. See Chapter 5.2 (Filing a Motion). The motion should set forth the reason or reasons why the Board should permit the moving party to supplement the original brief. (For example, if a motion to file a supplemental brief is based on a change in the law, the moving party would identify that change and argue the significance of the new authority to the appeal.)

(h) Reply Briefs — The Board does not normally accept briefs outside the time set in the briefing schedule, including any brief filed by the appealing party in reply to the response brief of the opposing party. See subsection (f), above.

The Board may, in its discretion, consider an appealing party's "reply brief" when the following conditions are met: (i) the brief is accompanied by a "MOTION TO ACCEPT REPLY BRIEF," (ii) the motion is premised upon and asserts surprise at the assertions of the other party, (iii) the brief identifies and challenges the assertions of the other party, and (iv) the motion and brief are filed with the Board within 21 days of the filing of the other party's brief. The brief should comply generally with the rules for motions. See Chapter 5.2 (Filing a Motion). If the appeal was filed by a detained respondent, see Chapter 4.7(a)(2) (Detained cases).

The Board will not suspend or delay adjudication of the appeal in anticipation of, or in response to, the filing of a reply brief.

(i) Amicus Curiae Briefs — Amicus curiae briefs are subject to the same rules as parties' briefs. See Chapter 4.6 (Appeal Briefs), 4.7 (Briefing Deadlines). The filing of multiple coordinated briefs from different amici that raise similar points is disfavored. Rather, prospective amici should submit a joint brief along with the request to appear. See generally Chapter 2.10 (Amicus Curiae). In addition, the Board may, at its discretion, acknowledge helpful amicus curiae brief(s) and contributors.

4.7   Briefing Deadlines

(a) Due Date — In appropriate cases, the Board sets briefing schedules and informs the parties of their respective deadlines for filing briefs. See Chapter 4.2 (Process). A party may not file a brief beyond the deadline set in the briefing schedule unless the brief is filed with the appropriate motion. See Chapter 4.6(g) (Supplemental Briefs), 4.6(h) (Reply Briefs), 4.7(d) (Untimely Briefs). Briefs must be submitted in accordance with the rules for timely filings at Chapter 3.1(b) (Must be "Timely").

(1) Non-detained cases — When the respondent is not detained, the parties are generally granted 21 calendar days each, sequentially, to file their initial briefs. See Chapter 3.1(b)(1) (Construction of "day"). The appealing party is provided 21 days from the date of the briefing schedule notice to file an appeal brief, and the opposing party will have an additional 21 days (marked from the date the appealing party's brief was due) in which to file a response brief. 8 C.F.R. § 1003.3(c)(1).

If both parties file an appeal (i.e. cross-appeals), then both parties are granted the same 21-day period in which to file an appeal brief. See 8 C.F.R. § 1003.3(c)(1). If either party wishes to reply to the appeal brief of the other, that party should comply with the rules for reply briefs. See Chapter 4.6(h) (Reply Briefs).

(2) Detained cases — When an appeal is filed in the case of a detained respondent, the respondent and DHS are both given the same 21 calendar days in which to file their initial briefs. The Board will accept reply briefs filed by DHS or by the respondent within 14 days after expiration of the briefing schedule. However, the Board will not suspend or delay adjudication of the appeal in anticipation of, or in response to, the filing of a reply brief. See Chapter 4.6(h) (Reply Briefs).

(3) Federal court remands — If a briefing schedule is set, the parties are both given the same 21 calendar days in which to file their initial briefs. If either party wishes to reply to the appeal brief of the other, that party should comply with the rules for reply briefs. See Chapter 4.6(h) (Reply Briefs). The Board, however, will not suspend or delay adjudication of the appeal in anticipation of, or in response to the filing of a reply brief.

(b) Processing — If a brief arrives at the Board and is timely, the brief is added to the record of proceedings and considered in the course of the adjudication of the appeal. If a brief arrives at the Board and is untimely, the brief is rejected and returned to the sender. See Chapter 3.1(c)(1) (Meaning of "rejected"). The Board may reject a brief as untimely at any time prior to the final adjudication of the appeal.

The Board does not issue receipts for briefs. If a party wishes to confirm the Board's receipt of a brief, the party should call the Automated Case Information Hotline for that information or, in the alternative, contact the Clerk's Office. See Chapter 1.6(b) (Telephone Calls), Appendix A (Directory), Appendix H (Hotlines). If a party wishes to document the Board's receipt of a brief, the party should either (i) save proof of delivery (such as a courier's delivery confirmation or a return receipt from the U.S. Postal Service) or (ii) request a conformed copy. See Chapter 3.1(d)(3) (Conformed copies).

(c) Extensions — The Board has the authority to set briefing deadlines and to extend them. A motion to request an extension of the briefing deadline needs to comply with the general rules and procedures for motions and filing. See Chapter 3 (Filing with the Board), Chapter 5.2 (Filing a Motion). The filing of an extension request does not automatically extend the filing deadline, nor can the filing party assume that a request will be granted. Until such time as the Board affirmatively grants an extension request, the existing deadline stands.

(1) Policy — In the interest of fairness and the efficient use of administrative resources, extension requests are not favored. A briefing deadline must be met unless the Board expressly extends it. There is no automatic entitlement to an extension of the briefing schedule by either party. If an extension request is denied, a motion to reconsider such denial will not be considered by the Board.

(A) Non-detained cases — It is the Board's policy to grant one briefing extension per party, if requested in a timely fashion. When a briefing extension is granted, the Board's policy is to grant an additional 21 days to file a brief regardless of the amount of time requested. The 21 days are added to the original filing deadline. Extensions are not calculated from the date the request was made or the date the request was received. It is also the Board's policy *not* to grant second briefing extension requests. Second requests are granted only in extraordinary circumstances not foreseeable at the time the first request was made (e.g., death, serious illness or medical condition, natural or manmade disaster).

(B) Detained cases — It is the Board's policy to grant one briefing extension per case, if requested in a timely fashion. If a briefing extension is granted, the Board's policy is to grant an additional 21 days to file a brief regardless of the amount of time requested. The 21 days are added to the original filing deadline and applies to both parties. Extensions are not calculated from the date the request was made or the date the request was received. It is also the Board's policy *not* to grant second briefing extension requests. Second requests are granted only in extraordinary circumstances not foreseeable at the time the first request was made (e.g., death, serious illness, natural or manmade disaster).

(2) Request deadline — Extension requests must be received by the Board by the brief's original due date. Extension requests received after the due date will not be granted.

The timely filing of an extension request does not relieve the requesting party of the obligation to meet the filing deadline. Until the extension request is affirmatively granted by the Board, the original deadline remains in effect. If an extension request is denied, a motion to reconsider such denial will not be considered by the Board.

(3) Duty to avoid delay — All parties have an ethical obligation to avoid delay. The Board's deadlines are designed to provide ample opportunity for filing, and a conscientious party should be able to meet these deadlines.

(4) Contents — Extension requests should be labeled "BRIEFING EXTENSION REQUEST" and be captioned accordingly. See Appendix E (Cover Pages). An extension request should indicate clearly:

- when the brief is due

- the reason for requesting an extension

- a representation that the party has exercised due diligence to meet the current deadline

- that the party will meet a revised deadline

- Proof of Service upon the other party

(d) Untimely Briefs — If a party wishes the Board to consider a brief despite its untimeliness, the brief should be accompanied by a written motion entitled "MOTION TO ACCEPT LATE-FILED BRIEF" and comply generally with the rules and procedures for motions and filings. See Chapter 3 (Filing with the Board), Chapter 5.2 (Filing a Motion). If the motion is filed without the brief, the brief will be rejected. See Chapter 3.1(c)(1) (Meaning of "rejected"). Thus, the motion and the brief need to be submitted together.

The Board has the discretion to consider a late-filed brief. Motions to accept a late-filed brief are not favored. If no request to extend the briefing schedule has been previously made, such motion to accept late-filed brief will only be granted upon the showing of good cause for failing to meet the briefing deadline. In all other cases, the moving party must demonstrate extraordinary circumstances (e.g., death, serious illness, natural or manmade disaster) to warrant a favorable exercise of discretion. A motion to accept late-filed brief should set forth in detail the reasons for the untimeliness, and the motion should be supported by affidavits, declarations, or other evidence. If the motion is granted, the motion and brief are incorporated into the record, and the brief is considered by the Board. If the motion is denied, the motion is retained as part of the record, but the brief is removed without consideration. In either case, the parties are notified of the Board's decision on the motion.

Parties may file a motion to accept a late-filed brief only once. Subsequent late-filed brief motions will not be considered. Motions to reconsider denials of late-filed brief motions will also not be considered.

(e) Decision not to File a Brief — If a party indicates on a Notice of Appeal (Form EOIR-26) that a brief will be filed but later decides not to file a brief, that party should notify the Board in writing *before* the date the brief is due. The filing should have a cover page clearly labeled "BRIEFING WAIVER" and expressly indicate that the party will not be filing a brief. See Appendix E (Cover Pages).

Failure to file a brief after an extension request has been granted is highly disfavored. See Chapter 4.16 (Summary Dismissal).

(f) Failure to File a Brief — When a party indicates on the Notice of Appeal (Form EOIR-26) that they will file a brief and thereafter fails to file a brief and fails to explain the failure to do so, the Board may summarily dismiss the appeal on that basis. 8 C.F.R. § 1003.1(d)(2)(i)(E). See Chapter 4.16 (Summary Dismissal).

4.8   Evidence on Appeal

(a) Record Evidence — The Board considers only that evidence that was admitted in the proceedings below.

(b) New Evidence on Appeal — The Board does not consider new evidence on appeal. If new evidence is submitted, that submission may be deemed a motion to remand proceedings to the immigration judge for consideration of that evidence and treated accordingly. 8 C.F.R. § 1003.1(d)(3)(iv). See Chapter 5.8 (Motions to Remand).

(c) Administrative Notice on Appeal — The Board may, at its discretion, take administrative notice of commonly known facts not appearing in the record. 8 C.F.R. § 1003.1(d)(3)(iv). For example, the Board may take administrative notice of current events and contents of official documents, such as country condition reports prepared by the U.S. Department of State.

(d) Representations of Practitioners — Representations made by practitioners in a brief or motion are not evidence. *Matter of Ramirez-Sanchez*, 17 I&N Dec. 503 (BIA 1980).

4.9   New Authorities Subsequent to Appeal

Whenever a party discovers new authority subsequent to the filing of a Notice of Appeal or brief, whether that authority supports or detracts from the party's arguments, that party should notify the Board of the new authority. See Chapter 4.6(g)(1) (New authorities). If either party wishes to brief new authority, that party should consult Chapter 4.6(g)(2) (New argument).

4.10   Combining and Separating Appeals

(a) **Consolidated Appeals** — Consolidation of appeals is the administrative joining of separate appeals into a single adjudication for all the parties involved. Consolidation is generally limited to appeals involving immediate family members, although the Board may consolidate other appeals where the cases are sufficiently interrelated.

Most of the consolidated cases before the Board were consolidated by the immigration judge in the proceedings below. The Board may consolidate appeals at its discretion or upon request of one or both of the parties, when appropriate. For example, the Board may grant consolidation when spouses or siblings have separate but overlapping circumstances or claims for relief. Consolidation must be sought through the filing of a written request that states the reasons for requesting consolidation. Such a request should include a cover page labeled "REQUEST FOR CONSOLIDATION OF APPEALS." See Appendix E (Cover Pages). A copy of the request should be filed for each case included in the request for consolidation. The request should be filed as soon as possible.

(b) **Concurrent Consideration of Appeals** — Concurrent consideration is the adjudication of unrelated appeals in tandem for the purposes of consistent adjudication and administrative efficiency. The Board may concurrently consider unrelated appeals at its discretion or upon request of one or both of the parties. Concurrent consideration must be sought through the filing of a written request that states the reasons for concurrent consideration. Such a request should include a cover page labeled "REQUEST FOR CONCURRENT CONSIDERATION OF APPEALS." See Appendix E (Cover Pages). Concurrent consideration differs from consolidated appeals in that, however similar the case or the adjudications, the appeals remain separate and distinct from one another. Concurrent consideration is appropriate, for example, when unrelated cases involve the same legal issue.

(c) **Severance of Appeals** — Severance of appeals is the division of a consolidated appeal into separate appeals, relative to each individual involved. The Board may sever appeals at its discretion or upon request of one or both of the parties. See *Matter of Taerghodsi*, 16 I&N Dec. 260 (BIA 1977). Severance must be sought through the filing of a written request that states the reasons for requesting severance. Such a request should include a cover page labeled "REQUEST FOR SEVERANCE OF APPEALS." See Appendix E (Cover Pages). Parties are advised, however, that such a request must be clear and filed as soon as possible.

4.11   Withdrawing an Appeal

(a) **Procedure** — An appealing party may, at any time prior to the entry of a decision by the Board, voluntarily withdraw their appeal, with or without the consent of the opposing party. The withdrawal must be in writing and filed with the Board. The cover page to the withdrawal should be labeled "MOTION TO WITHDRAW APPEAL" and comply with the requirements for filing. See Chapter 3 (Filing with the Board), Appendix E (Cover Pages).

(b) Untimely Withdrawal — If a withdrawal is not received by the Board prior to the Board's rendering of a decision, the withdrawal will not be recognized, and the Board's decision will become binding.

(c) Effect of Withdrawal — When an appeal is withdrawn, the decision of the immigration judge becomes immediately final and binding as if no appeal had ever been filed, and the respondent is then subject to the immigration judge's original decision. See 8 C.F.R. § 1003.4. Thus, if the respondent appeals an immigration judge's order of removal or deportation, and then withdraws the appeal, the DHS may at that point remove or deport the respondent. If the respondent appeals an immigration judge's order in which the respondent was granted voluntary departure, and then withdraws the appeal, the period of voluntary departure runs from the date of the immigration judge's decision, not the date of the appeal's withdrawal.

(d) Distinction from Motion to Remand — Parties should not confuse a motion to withdraw appeal with a motion to remand. The two motions are distinct from one another and have very different consequences. While a motion to withdraw appeal is filed by a party who chooses to accept the decision of the immigration judge, a motion to remand is filed by a party who wants the case returned to the immigration judge for further consideration. See Chapter 5.8 (Motions to Remand).

(e) Represented Respondents — If a represented respondent wishes to withdraw an appeal, the respondent's practitioner of record should file the withdrawal. If a represented respondent insists on filing the withdrawal without the assistance of their practitioner of record, the withdrawal should indicate whether it is being made with the advice and consent of the practitioner of record. The withdrawal should also be filed with Proof of Service on the respondent's practitioner of record. See Chapter 3.2(d) (Proof of Service), Appendix F (Cert. of Service).

4.12 Non-Opposition to Appeal

(a) Failure to Oppose — The failure of the opposing party to affirmatively oppose an appeal does not automatically result in the appeal being sustained. While the Board may consider the opposing party's silence in adjudicating the appeal, the silence does not dictate the disposition of the appeal.

(b) Express Non-opposition — The opposing party may affirmatively express non-opposition to an appeal at any time prior to the entry of a decision by the Board. Such non-opposition should be expressed either in the response to the appeal or in the form of a notice labeled "NON-OPPOSITION TO APPEAL" and should be properly served on the other party. See Chapter 3.2 (Service), Appendix E (Cover Pages). While the Board may weigh the opposing party's non-opposition in adjudicating the appeal, that non-opposition does not dictate the disposition of the appeal.

(c) Withdrawal of Opposition — The opposing party may withdraw opposition to an appeal at any time prior to the entry of a decision by the Board. Such non-opposition should be expressed in the form of a notice labeled "WITHDRAWAL OF OPPOSITION TO APPEAL" and be properly served on the other party. See Chapter 3.2 (Service), Appendix E (Cover Pages). While the Board may weigh the opposing party's withdrawal of opposition in adjudication of the appeal, that withdrawal does not dictate that disposition of the appeal.

4.13   Effect of Departure

(a) Respondent's Appeal — Departure from the United States can jeopardize a respondent's right to appeal, even when the departure is authorized or compelled by DHS. Departure from the United States prior to filing an appeal may be construed as a waiver of the right to appeal. Departure from the United States while an appeal is pending may be construed as a withdrawal of that appeal. See 8 C.F.R. §§ 1003.3(e), 1003.4.

(b) DHS Appeal — The respondent's departure from the United States while a DHS appeal is pending does not constitute a withdrawal of the DHS appeal, nor does it render the DHS appeal moot.

4.14   Interlocutory Appeals

(a) Nature of Interlocutory Appeals — Most appeals are filed *after* the immigration judge issues a final decision in the case. In contrast, an interlocutory appeal asks the Board to review a ruling by the immigration judge before the immigration judge issues a final decision.

(b) Bond Appeals — Bond appeals should not be confused with interlocutory appeals. There are separate rules for bond appeals. See Chapter 7 (Bond).

(c) Scope of Interlocutory Appeals — The Board does not normally entertain interlocutory appeals and generally limits interlocutory appeals to instances involving either important jurisdictional questions regarding the administration of the immigration laws or recurring questions in the handling of cases by immigration judges. See *Matter of K-*, 20 I&N Dec. 418 (BIA 1991).

(d) Filing an Interlocutory Appeal — Interlocutory appeals should be timely filed on a Notice of Appeal (Form EOIR-26). Next to the words "What decision are you appealing?" in box 5, type or write in the words "INTERLOCUTORY APPEAL." Do not check any of the three options in box 5. The appeal must indicate the date of the immigration judge's decision, the precise nature and disposition of that decision, and the precise issue being appealed. If the interlocutory appeal is based upon a written decision, a copy of that decision should be included with the appeal.

(e) Briefing — The Board does not normally issue briefing schedules for interlocutory appeals. If an appealing party wishes to file a brief, the brief should accompany the Notice of Appeal or be promptly submitted after the Notice of Appeal is filed. If an opposing party wishes to file a brief, the brief should be filed as soon as possible after the appeal is filed. The Board will not, however, suspend or delay adjudication of an interlocutory appeal in anticipation of, or in response to, the filing of a brief.

4.15   Summary Affirmance

Under certain circumstances, the Board may affirm, without opinion, the decision of an immigration judge or DHS officer. The Board may affirm a decision if all of these conditions are met:

- the immigration judge or DHS decision reached the correct result

- any errors in the decision were harmless or nonmaterial

- either (a) the issues on appeal are squarely controlled by existing Board or federal court precedent and do not involve the application of a precedent to a novel factual situation, or (b) the factual and legal issues raised on appeal are not so substantial that the case warrants the issuance of a written opinion

See 8 C.F.R § 1003.1(e)(4). By regulation, a summary affirmance order reads: "The Board affirms, without opinion, the result of the decision below. The decision below is, therefore, the final agency determination. See 8 C.F.R. § 3.1(e)(4)." 8 C.F.R. § 1003.1(e)(4)(ii).

A summary affirmance order will not contain further explanation or reasoning. Such an order approves the result reached by the immigration judge or DHS. Summary affirmance does not mean that the Board approves of all the reasoning of that decision, but it does reflect that any errors in the decision were considered harmless or not material to the outcome of the case. See 8 C.F.R. § 1003.1(e)(4).

Note that any motion to reconsider or motion to reopen filed after a summary affirmance order should be filed with the Board. See Chapters 5.6 (Motions to Reopen) and 5.7 (Motions to Reconsider). However, by regulation, the Board cannot entertain a motion based solely on an argument that the case should not have been affirmed without opinion. See 8 C.F.R. § 1003.2(b)(3).

4.16   Summary Dismissal

(a) Nature of "Summary" Dismissal — Under certain circumstances, the Board is authorized to dismiss an appeal without reaching its merits. See 8 C.F.R. § 1003.1(d)(2)(i).

(b) Failure to Specify Grounds for Appeal — When a party takes an appeal, the Notice of Appeal (Form EOIR-26) must identify the reasons for the appeal. A party should be specific and detailed in stating the grounds of the appeal, specifically identifying the finding of fact, the conclusions of law, or both, that are being challenged. 8 C.F.R. § 1003.3(b). An appeal, or any portion of an appeal, may be summarily dismissed if the Notice of Appeal (Form EOIR-26), and any brief or attachment, fails to adequately inform the Board of the specific reasons for the appeal. 8 C.F.R. § 1003.1(d)(2)(i)(A).

(c) Failure to File a Brief — An appeal may be summarily dismissed if the Notice of Appeal (Form EOIR-26) indicates that a brief or statement will be filed in support of the appeal, but no brief, statement, or explanation for not filing a brief is filed within the briefing deadline. 8 C.F.R. § 1003.1(d)(2)(i)(E). See Chapter 4.7(e) (Decision not to File a Brief).

(d) Other Grounds for Summary Dismissal — An appeal can also be summarily dismissed for the following reasons:

- the appeal is based on a finding of fact or conclusion of law that has already been conceded by the appealing party

- the appeal is from an order granting the relief requested

- the appeal is filed for an improper purpose

- the appeal does not fall within the Board's jurisdiction

- the appeal is untimely

- the appeal is barred by an affirmative waiver of the right of appeal

- the appeal fails to meet essential statutory or regulatory requirements

- the appeal is expressly prohibited by statute or regulation

See 8 C.F.R. § 1003.1(d)(2)(i).

(e) Sanctions — Practitioners are admonished that the filing of an appeal that is summarily dismissed may be deemed frivolous behavior and may result in discipline. 8 C.F.R. § 1003.1(d)(2)(iii). See Chapters 4.17 (Frivolous Appeals), 11 (Discipline).

4.17   Frivolous Appeals

If it appears to the Board, at any time, that an appeal is filed for an improper purpose or to cause unnecessary delay, the appeal may be dismissed. See 8 C.F.R. § 1003.1(d)(2)(i)(D). The filing of a frivolous appeal may be grounds for discipline against a practitioner. See Chapter 11.4 (Conduct).

4.18   Certification by an Immigration Judge

An immigration judge may ask the Board to review their decision. 8 C.F.R. § 1003.7. To "certify" a case to the Board, an immigration court serves a notice of certification on the parties. That notice informs the parties that the case has been certified and sets a briefing schedule.

The right to appeal is separate and distinct from certification. To safeguard the opportunity to appeal and be heard by the Board, parties should file an appeal even if an immigration judge has certified the case. 8 C.F.R. § 1003.3(d).

4.19   Federal Court Remands

(a) Nature of Federal Court Remands — The decisions of the Board are reviewable in certain federal courts, depending on the nature of the appeal. Where an appeal is taken from a Board decision regarding of an immigration judge's ruling, the federal court may remand the case back to the Board for further proceedings. For example, the federal court may remand to allow the Board to consider our prior decision because of a change in law or ask the Board to re-examine our prior decision in light of the court's rulings.

(b) Notification — When the Board receives notification of a federal court's order from the Office of Immigration Litigation (OIL) or the United States Attorney's Office, a written notification is sent to both the respondent and DHS.

(c) Notice of Appearance — If a party is represented by a practitioner, the practitioner must submit a Notice of Entry of Appearance as Attorney or Representative Before the Board of Immigration Appeals (Form EOIR-27) to become the practitioner of record on remand. See Chapter 4.3(c) (Representation). Registered attorneys and fully accredited representatives must electronically file their Notice of Appearance (Form EOIR-27) through ECAS in cases eligible for electronic filing. If the submission of the Form EOIR-27 precedes issuance of notification of a federal court remand, the submission may be rejected.

(d) Briefing and Transcript — In appropriate cases, a briefing schedule is provided to both parties and informs the parties of their respective deadlines for filing briefs. If a briefing schedule is set, the parties are both given the same 21 calendar days in which to file their initial briefs. See Chapter 4.7(a) (Due Date). Filing guidance can be found Chapter 3 (Filing with the Board) and Chapter 4.2(e) (Briefing Schedule), 4.6 (Appeal Briefs), 4.7(c) (Extensions). Also, in appropriate cases, a transcript is sent to the parties along with the briefing schedule. See Chapter 4.2(f) (Transcription).

4.20   ABC Settlement

(a) ABC Class Members — Members of the class covered by the ABC Settlement Agreement, who timely registered to receive benefits under the agreement (either by applying directly or by applying for TPS, if Salvadoran) may be entitled to certain rights and benefits pursuant to the agreement. See *American Baptist Churches v. Thornburgh*, 760 F. Supp. 796 (N.D. Cal. 1991). ABC class members include Salvadorans who entered the United States on or before September 19, 1990, and Guatemalans who entered the United States on or before October 1, 1990.[1]

(b) Certain El Salvador and Guatemala Nationals — Section 203 of the Nicaraguan Adjustment and Central American Relief Act ("NACARA") provides that certain nationals of El Salvador and Guatemala are eligible to apply for suspension of deportation, or NACARA cancellation, under standards similar to those in effect prior to the enactment of the Illegal Immigration Reform and Immigrant Responsibility Act ("IIRIRA"). Pub. L. No. 105-100, 111 Stat. 2160 (1997).

To qualify for NACARA relief as a Salvadoran or Guatemalan national, the applicant must have either:

- filed an application for asylum on or before April 1, 1990; or

---

[1] Administrative closure was expressly authorized for certain ABC class members in order to implement the ABC settlement agreement and provide such class members the opportunity to exercise their rights under the agreement. *See* 8 C.F.R. §§ 1240.62(b) and 1240.70(f)-(h); *ABC*, 760 F. Supp. at 805; *Matter of Castro-Tum*, 27 I&N Dec. 271, 276–77 (2018)

- registered for benefits under *American Baptist Churches v. Thornburgh*, 760 F. Supp. 796 (N.D. Cal. 1991) and not been apprehended at the time of entry if such entry occurred after December 19, 1990. 8 C.F.R. § 1240.61(a)(1)-(2).

A Salvadoran national is considered to have registered for *ABC* benefits if they entered the United States on or before September 19, 1990, and either applied for temporary protected status on or before October 31, 1991, or submitted an ABC registration form on or before October 31, 1991. *Id.* § 1240.60(1). A Guatemalan national is considered to have registered for *ABC* benefits if they entered the United States on or before October 1, 1990, and submitted an ABC registration form on or before December 31, 1991. 8 C.F.R. § 1240.60(2).

(c) Board Role — The Board will not evaluate whether a class member is eligible for a *de novo* asylum adjudication before an Asylum Officer. Rather, DHS's U.S. Citizenship and Immigration Services is assigned the role of making substantive determinations of an applicant's eligibility.

Chapter 5 Motions before the Board

5.1   Who May File

(a) Parties — Only a respondent who is the subject of an underlying appeal before the Board, the respondent's practitioner of record, or DHS may file a motion. See Chapter 2.1(b)(7) (Filings After Entry of Appearance as Practitioner of Record). An unrepresented or pro se party may receive assistance from a practitioner with the drafting, completion, or filling in of blank spaces of a specific motion intended to be filed with the Board pursuant to a limited appearance for document assistance. See Chapter 2.1(c) (Limited Appearance for Document Assistance); 3.3(b) (Signatures).

A motion must identify all parties covered by the motion and state clearly their full names and A-numbers, including all family members. See Appendix E (Cover Pages). The Board will *not* assume that a motion includes all family members (or group members in a consolidated proceeding). See Chapter 4.10 (Combining and Separating Appeals).

(b) Practitioners — Motions may be filed either by a party, if unrepresented ("pro se"), or by a party's practitioner of record. See Chapter 2 (Appearances before the Board). Whenever a party is represented, the party should submit all motions to the Board through the practitioner of record. See Chapter 2.1(b)(7) (Filings After Entry of Appearance as Practitioner of Record).

(1) Motions to reopen and motions to reconsider — A practitioner must file a Notice of Appearance (Form EOIR-27) with motions to reopen and motions to reconsider to be the practitioner of record on the motion, even if the practitioner is already the practitioner of record in proceedings before the Board. See Chapter 2.1(b) (Entering an Appearance as the Practitioner of Record).

(2) All other motions — On any motion that is not a motion to reopen or a motion to reconsider, if a practitioner is already the practitioner of record, the motion need not be accompanied by a Notice of Appearance (Form EOIR-27). However, if a practitioner is appearing for the first time and seeks to be the practitioner of record on the motion, the practitioner must file a Form EOIR-27 along with that motion. See Chapter 2.1(b) (Entering an Appearance as the Practitioner of Record).

(3) Practitioner document assistance to unrepresented respondent with motions — An unrepresented or pro se party may receive assistance from a practitioner with the drafting, completion, or filling in of blank spaces of a specific motion intended to be filed with the Board pursuant to a limited appearance for document assistance. When filed, the motion must be accompanied by a Notice of Limited Appearance (Form EOIR-60). See Chapter 2.1(c) (Limited Appearance for Document Assistance).

(c) Persons not Party to the Proceeding — Only a party to a proceeding, or a party's practitioner of record, may file a motion pertaining to that proceeding. An unrepresented or pro se party may receive assistance from a practitioner with the drafting, completion, or filling in of blank spaces of a specific motion intended to be filed with the Board pursuant to a limited appearance for document assistance. See Chapter 2.1(c) (Limited Appearance for Document Assistance); 3.3(b) (Signatures). Family members, employers, and other third parties may not file a motion. If a third party seeks Board action in a particular case, the request should be made through one of the parties. Third parties who wish to appear as amicus curiae should consult Chapter 2.10 (Amicus Curiae).

5.2   Filing a Motion

(a) Jurisdiction — Motions must be filed in the right place. See Appendix J (Filing Motions). The Board may entertain motions only in those cases in which it has jurisdiction.

(1) Cases never before the Board — The Board cannot entertain motions for cases that have never been before it. Cases "never before the Board" include both appeals that were never filed and appeals that were rejected for a filing defect that was never remedied.

(2) Cases pending before the Board — Where an appeal is pending before the Board, all motions regarding that appeal should be filed with the Board.

(3) Cases already decided by the Board —

(A) Motions to reopen and motion to reconsider — As a general rule, where an appeal has been decided by the Board and no case is currently pending, a motion to reopen or a motion to reconsider may be filed with the Board. See Chapters 5.6 (Motions to Reopen), 5.7 (Motions to Reconsider). Parties should be mindful of the strict time and number limits on motions to reopen and motions to reconsider. See Chapters 5.6(c) (Time Limits), 5.6(d) (Number Limits), 5.7(c) (Time Limits), 5.7(d) (Number Limits).

(B) Motions subsequent to remand — Once a case has been remanded to the immigration judge, the only motion that the Board will entertain is a motion to reconsider the decision to remand. All other motions must be filed with the immigration judge. Motions to reconsider a remand order are not favored, and concerns regarding the decision to remand should be presented to the immigration judge.

(C) Motions on appeals dismissed for lack of jurisdiction — Where an appeal has been dismissed for lack of jurisdiction, the Board cannot consider a motion to reopen. See *Matter of Mladineo*, 14 I&N Dec. 591 (BIA 1974). The only motion that the Board may entertain is a motion to reconsider the Board's finding that it lacks jurisdiction.

(D) Motions on appeals dismissed as untimely — Where an appeal has been dismissed as untimely, the Board does not have jurisdiction to consider a motion to reopen. The only motion that the Board may entertain is a motion to reconsider the Board's finding that the appeal was untimely. See *Matter of Lopez*, 22 I&N Dec. 16 (BIA 1998).

(E) Motion on appeals affirmed without opinion — By regulation, the Board cannot entertain a motion based solely on an argument that the case should not have been affirmed without opinion. See Chapter 4.15 (Summary Affirmance). Otherwise, the Board retains jurisdiction over any motion to reconsider or motion to reopen filed after a summary affirmance order. See Chapters 5.6 (Motions to Reopen) and 5.7 (Motions to Reconsider).

(b) Form — There is no official form for filing a motion before the Board. Motions should not be filed on a Notice of Appeal (Form EOIR-26), which is used exclusively for the filing of appeals.

Motions and supporting documents must comply with the general rules and procedures for filing. See Chapter 3 (Filing with the Board). The Board prefers that motions and supporting documents be assembled in a certain order. See Chapter 3.3(c)(1)(B) (Motions).

A motion should be characterized and labeled as accurately as possible. The Board construes a motion according to its content, not its title, and applies time and number limits accordingly. See Chapter 5.3 (Motion Limits).

Motions should clearly contain all pertinent information, and the Board recommends that parties use captions containing the following material:

- title (Example: "Respondent's Motion to Reopen")

- the full name (as it appears on the charging document) for each respondent included in the motion

- the A-number for each respondent involved in the motion

- the type of hearing or adjudication underlying the motion (e.g., removal, deportation, exclusion, bond, visa petition)

- the adjudicator whose decision underlies the motion (e.g., the immigration court, the DHS officer, or the Board), where appropriate

All motions must be made in writing, signed, and served on all parties. The manner of completion of service of documents on the opposing party depends on whether both parties are participating in ECAS, as explained in Chapter 3.2 (Service). A motion must identify *all* persons included in the motion. See Chapter 5.1(a) (Parties). A motion must state with particularity the grounds on which it is based and must identify the relief or remedy sought by the moving party.

If a motion involves a detained or incarcerated respondent, the motion should clearly state that information. The Board recommends that the cover page to the motion be prominently marked "DETAINED" in the upper right corner and highlighted, if possible. See Appendix E (Cover Pages).

(c) Proof of Service — All motions must be served on the other party and must contain Proof of Service. See Chapter 3.2 (Service), Appendix F (Cert. of Service).

(d) Motion Fee and Fee Waivers — Where required, a motion must be accompanied by the appropriate filing fee, fee receipt, or Fee Waiver Request (Form EOIR-26A). See Chapter 3.4 (Filing Fees).

(e) Copy of Underlying Order — Motions to reopen and motions to reconsider should be accompanied by a copy of the Board's order.

(f) Evidence — Statements made in a motion are not evidence. If a motion is predicated upon evidence that was not made part of the record by the immigration judge, that evidence should be submitted with the motion. Such evidence includes sworn affidavits, declarations under the penalty of perjury, and documentary evidence. The Board will not suspend or delay adjudication of a motion pending the receipt of supplemental evidence.

Any material that is not in the English language must be accompanied by a certified English translation. 8 C.F.R. §§ 1003.2(g)(1), 1003.33. See Chapter 3.3(a) (Language). Documents regarding criminal convictions must comport with the requirements set forth in 8 C.F.R. § 1003.41.

(g) Application for Relief — A motion based upon eligibility for relief must be accompanied by a copy of the application for that relief, if an application is normally required. See 8 C.F.R. § 1003.2(c)(1).

The application for relief must be duly completed and executed in accordance with the requirements for such relief. The original of an application for relief is generally not required but should be held by the filing party for submission to the immigration judge or DHS following the Board's ruling on the motion. See Chapter 12.3 (Submitting Completed Forms). The copy that is submitted to the Board should be accompanied by a copy of the appropriate supporting documents.

If a certain form of relief requires an application, *prima facie eligibility for that relief cannot be shown without it*. For example, if a motion to reopen is based on adjustment of status, a copy of the application for that relief (Form I-485) should be filed *with* the motion, along with the necessary documents. See subsection (h), below.

Application fees are not paid to the Board and should not accompany the motion. Fees for applications should be paid if and when the case is remanded to the immigration judge in accordance with the filing procedures for that application. See Chapter 3.4(i) (Application Fees).

(h) Visa Petitions — If a motion is based on adjustment of status and there is an underlying visa petition that has been approved, evidence of the approved visa petition should accompany the motion. When a petition is subject to visa availability, evidence that a visa is immediately available to the beneficiary should also accompany the motion (e.g., a copy of the State Department's Visa Bulletin reflecting that the petition is "current").

If a motion is based on adjustment of status and the underlying visa petition has not yet been adjudicated, a copy of that visa petition should accompany the motion. If the visa petition has already been filed with DHS, evidence of that filing should accompany the motion.

Parties are advised that, in certain instances, an approved visa petition is required. See e.g., *Matter of H-A-*, 22 I&N Dec. 728 (BIA 1999), modified by *Matter of Velarde*, 23 I&N Dec. 253 (BIA 2002).

Filing fees for visa petitions are not paid to the Board and should not accompany the motion. The filing fee for a visa petition is submitted to DHS when the petition is filed with DHS.

(i) Oral Argument — The Board generally does not grant requests for oral argument on a motion. See Chapter 8.2(b) (Motions).

(j) Draft Orders — Parties should not include draft orders in the motion filing. The Board always issues its own order.

(k) Confirmation of Receipt — The Board issues filing receipts for motions to reopen and motions to reconsider. The Board does not issue filing receipts for other types of motions. See Chapter 3.1(d) (Filing Receipts). The Board will, however, return a conformed copy of a filed motion if it complies with Chapter 3.1(d)(3) (Conformed copies).

5.3   Motion Limits

Certain motions are limited in time (when the motion must be filed) and number (how many motions may be filed). Motions to reopen and motions to reconsider are limited in both time and number. See Chapters 5.6 (Motion to Reopen), 5.7 (Motions to Reconsider). Motions to accept a late-filed brief are limited in number. See Chapter 4.7(d) (Untimely Briefs). These time and number limits are strictly enforced.

A compound motion is a motion that combines a motion to reopen or a motion to reconsider with another motion (or with each other). Time and number limits on motions to reopen and motions to reconsider apply even when part of a compound motion, and the Board will consider only that portion of the motion that is not time or number barred. For example, if a motion seeks both reopening and reconsideration, and is filed more than 30 days after the Board's decision but within 90 days of that decision, the Board will entertain the portion of the motion that seeks reopening, but not the portion that seeks reconsideration.

5.4   Motion Briefs

A motion need not be supported by a brief. However, if a brief is filed, it should accompany the motion. See 8 C.F.R. § 1003.2(g)(3). A brief filed in opposition to a motion must be filed within 13 days from the date of service of the motion. 8 C.F.R. § 1003.2(g)(3).

Motion briefs should generally follow the filing requirements, writing guidelines, formatting requirements, and citation conventions set forth in Chapter 4.6 (Appeal

Briefs). Motion briefs should also comport with the requirements set out in Chapter 3.3 (Documents). The Board does not issue briefing schedules on motions.

5.5   Transcript Requests

The Board does not prepare a transcript of proceedings in response to a motion. If a party feels that a transcript is necessary, the party should file a motion articulating why a transcript is necessary. See generally Chapter 4.2(f) (Transcription).

Copies of digital audio or cassette tape recordings may be requested by the parties and their practitioner of record. A Freedom of Information Act (FOIA) request is not required. Parties may obtain a copy that is not prohibited (e.g., classified information, subject to protective order). Requests for copies may be made to the Board in person, by mail, or by email. The Board encourages parties to request a copy of the digitally- or cassette tape-recorded hearings by email using "EOIR.BIA.ROP.Requests@usdoj.gov." This email address is only to be used for requests for a copy of the official record or portion of the official record. The Board does not provide self-service copying. Alternatively, the parties may file a request pursuant to FOIA. See Chapters 1.5(e) (Records), 13 (Requesting Records).

For more information on digitally- or cassette-recorded hearings, parties should consult the Immigration Court Practice Manual, which is available on the EOIR website.

5.6   Motions to Reopen

(a) Purpose — A motion to reopen asks the Board to reopen proceedings in which the Board has already rendered a decision in order to consider new facts or evidence in the case.

(b) Requirements —

(1) Filing — Motions to reopen must comply with the general requirements for filing a motion. See Chapter 5.2 (Filing a Motion). Depending on the nature of the motion, a filing fee may be required. See Chapter 3.4 (Filing Fees).

(2) Content — A motion to reopen must state the new facts that will be proven at a reopened hearing, and the motion must be supported by affidavits or other evidentiary material. 8 C.F.R. § 1003.2(c)(1).

A motion to reopen will not be granted unless it appears to the Board that the evidence offered is material and was not available and could not have been discovered or presented at an earlier stage in the proceedings. See 8 C.F.R. § 1003.2(c)(1).

A motion to reopen based on an application for relief will not be granted if it appears the respondent's right to apply for that relief was fully explained and the respondent had an opportunity to apply for that relief at an earlier stage in the proceedings (unless the relief is sought on the basis of circumstances that have arisen subsequent to that stage of the proceedings). See 8 C.F.R. § 1003.2(c)(1).

(c) Time Limits — As a general rule, a motion to reopen must be filed within 90 days of the Board's final administrative decision. 8 C.F.R. § 1003.2(c)(2). (For cases decided by the Board before July 1, 1996, the motion to reopen was due on or before September 30, 1996. 8 C.F.R. § 1003.2(c)(2).) There are few exceptions. See subsection (e), below.

(d) Number Limits — A party is permitted only one motion to reopen. 8 C.F.R. § 1003.2(c)(2). There are few exceptions. See subsection (e), below.

(e) Exceptions to the Limits on Motions to Reopen — A motion to reopen may be filed outside the time and number limits in very specific circumstances. See 8 C.F.R. § 1003.2(c)(3).

(1) Changed circumstances — When a motion to reopen is based on a request for asylum, withholding or removal, or relief under the Convention Against Torture, and it is premised on new circumstances, the motion must contain a complete description of the new facts that comprise those circumstances and articulate how those circumstances affect the party's eligibility for relief. See 8 C.F.R. § 1003.2(c)(3)(ii). Motions based on changed circumstances must also be accompanied by evidence of the changed circumstances alleged. See 8 C.F.R. § 1003.2(c).

(2) In absentia proceedings — There are special rules pertaining to motions to reopen following a respondent's failure to appear for a hearing. An "in absentia" order (an order entered when the respondent did not come to the hearing) cannot be appealed to the Board. *Matter of Guzman*, 22 I&N Dec. 722 (BIA 1999). If a respondent misses a hearing and the immigration judge orders the respondent removed from the United States, the respondent must file a motion to reopen with the immigration judge, explaining why they missed the hearing. (Unlike the in absentia order, the immigration judge's ruling on the motion can be appealed.) Such motions are subject to strict deadlines under certain circumstances. See 8 C.F.R. §§ 1003.2(c)(3)(i), 1003.23(b)(4)(ii), 1003.23(b)(4)(iii).

(3) Joint motions — Motions that are agreed upon by all parties and are jointly filed are not limited in time or number. See 8 C.F.R. § 1003.2(c)(3)(iii).

(4) DHS motions — For cases in removal proceedings, DHS may not be subject to time and number limits on motions to reopen. See 8 C.F.R. § 1003.2(c)(2), (3). For cases brought in deportation or exclusion, DHS is subject to the time and number limits on motions to reopen, unless the basis of the motion is fraud in the original proceeding or a crime that would support termination of asylum. See 8 C.F.R. § 1003.2(c)(3)(iv).

(5) Pre-9/30/96 motions — Motions filed before September 30, 1996, do not count toward the one-motion limit.

(6) Battered spouses, children, and parents — There are special rules for certain motions to reopen by battered spouses, children, and parents. See Immigration and Nationality Act § 240(c)(7)(C)(iv).

(7) ECAS system outage (electronic filing) — System outages may occur that make electronic filing through ECAS unavailable and may impact filing deadlines for a case where electronic filing is mandatory. If EOIR determines that an unplanned outage has occurred, filing deadlines that occur on the last day for filing in a specific case will be extended until the first day of system availability that is not a Saturday, Sunday, or legal holiday. See 8 C.F.R. § 1003.2(g)(5). Note that planned system outages will not impact filing deadlines since these can be proactively addressed by the parties. EOIR will maintain an ECAS Outage Log that will note planned and unplanned ECAS system outages.

(8) Fee waiver denied — If a fee waiver request does not establish the inability to pay the required fee, the Board will grant 15 days to re-file the rejected motion with the filing fee or new fee waiver request. Any applicable filing deadlines will be tolled during this 15-day period. See 8 C.F.R. § 1003.8(a)(3). See Chapter 3.4 (Filing fees).

(9) Other — In addition to the regulatory exceptions for motions to reopen, exceptions may be created in accordance with special statutes, published case law, directives, or other special legal circumstances. The Board may also reopen proceedings at any time on its own initiative. 8 C.F.R. § 1003.2(a).

(f) Evidence — A motion to reopen must be supported by evidence. See Chapter 5.2(f) (Evidence).

(g) Motions Filed While an Appeal is Pending — Once an appeal is filed with the Board, the immigration judge no longer has jurisdiction over the case. See Chapter 4.2(a)(2) (Appeal to the Board vs. motion before the immigration judge). Thus, motions to reopen should not be filed with an immigration judge after an appeal is taken to the Board. A motion to reopen that is filed with the Board during the pendency of an appeal is generally treated as a motion to remand for further proceedings before an immigration judge. 8 C.F.R. § 1003.2(c)(4). See Chapter 5.8 (Motions to Remand).

(h) Administratively Closed Cases — When proceedings have been administratively closed, the proper motion is a motion to recalendar, *not* a motion to reopen. See Chapter 5.9(h) (Motion to Recalendar).

(i) Automatic Stays — A motion to reopen that is filed with the Board does not automatically stay an order of removal or deportation. See Chapter 6 (Stays and Expedite Requests).

(j) Criminal Convictions — A motion claiming that a criminal conviction has been overturned, vacated, modified, or disturbed in some way *must* be accompanied by clear evidence that the conviction *has actually been disturbed*. Thus, neither an intention to seek post-conviction relief nor the mere eligibility for post-conviction relief, without more, is sufficient to reopen proceedings.

5.7   Motions to Reconsider

(a) Purpose — A motion to reconsider either identifies an error in law or fact in a prior Board decision or identifies a change in law that affects a prior Board decision and asks the Board to re-examine its ruling. A motion to reconsider is based on the existing record and does not seek to introduce new facts or evidence.

(b) Requirements — Motions to reconsider must comply with the general requirements for filing a motion. See Chapter 5.2 (Filing a Motion). A filing fee, fee receipt, or a fee waiver request may be required. See Chapter 3.4 (Filing Fees).

(c) Time Limits — A motion to reconsider must be filed within 30 days of the Board's decision. 8 C.F.R. § 1003.2(b)(2). (For cases decided by the Board before July 1, 1996, the motion to reconsider was due on or before July 31, 1996.) 8 C.F.R. § 1003.2(b)(2).

(d) Number Limits — As a general rule, a party may file only one motion to reconsider. See 8 C.F.R. § 1003.2(b)(2). Motions filed prior to July 31, 1996, do not count toward the one-motion limit. Although a party may file a motion to reconsider the denial of a motion to reopen, a party may not file a motion to reconsider the denial of a motion to reconsider. 8 C.F.R. § 1003.2(b)(2).

(e) Summary Affirmance Orders — A motion to reconsider may not be based solely on an argument that an immigration judge's decision should not have been affirmed without opinion. See 8 C.F.R. § 1003.2(b)(3).

(f) Exceptions to the Limits on Motions to Reconsider —

(1) Respondent motions — There are no exceptions to the time and number limitations on motions to reconsider when filed by a respondent. However, if a fee waiver request does not establish the inability to pay the required fee, the Board will grant 15 days to re-file the rejected motion with the filing fee or new fee waiver request, and any applicable filing deadline is tolled during the 15-day cure period. See Chapter 3.4 (Filing fees), Chapter 5.6(e)(7) (Fee waiver denied).

(2) DHS motions — DHS motions to reconsider are subject to certain limitations. See 8 C.F.R. § 1003.2(b)(2).

(3) ECAS system outage (electronic filing) — System outages may occur that make electronic filing through ECAS unavailable and may impact filing deadlines for a case where electronic filing is mandatory. If EOIR determines that an unplanned outage has occurred, filing deadlines that occur on the last day for filing in a specific case will be extended until the first day of system availability that is not a Saturday, Sunday, or legal holiday. See 8 C.F.R. § 1003.2(g)(5). Note that planned system outages will not impact filing deadlines since these can be proactively addressed by the parties. EOIR will maintain an ECAS Outage Log that will note planned and unplanned ECAS system outages.

(4) Other — Exceptions to the time and number limits on motions to reconsider may be created by statute, published case law, or regulations. The Board may also reconsider proceedings at any time on its own initiative. 8 C.F.R. § 1003.2(a).

(g) Identification of Error — A motion to reconsider must state with particularity the errors of fact or law in the prior Board decision, with appropriate citation to authority and the record. If a motion to reconsider is premised upon changes in the law, the motion should identify the changes and, where appropriate, provide copies of that law. See Chapter 4.6(d)(6) (Statutes, rules, regulations, and other legal authorities and sources).

(h) Motions Filed While an Appeal is Pending — Once an appeal is filed with the Board, the immigration judge no longer has jurisdiction over the case. See Chapter 4.2(a)(2) (Appeal to the Board vs. motion before the immigration judge). Thus, motions to reconsider should not be filed with an immigration judge after an appeal is taken to the Board. A motion to reconsider that is filed with the Board during the pendency of an appeal is generally treated as a motion to remand for further proceedings before an immigration judge. 8 C.F.R. § 1003.2(b)(1). See Chapter 5.8 (Motions to Remand).

(i) Automatic Stays — A motion to reconsider does not automatically stay an order or removal or deportation. See Chapter 6 (Stays and Expedite Requests).

(j) Criminal Convictions — When a criminal conviction has been overturned, vacated, modified, or disturbed in some way, the proper motion is a motion to reopen, not a motion to reconsider. See Chapter 5.6(j) (Criminal Convictions).

5.8   Motions to Remand

(a) Purpose — A motion to remand seeks to return jurisdiction of a case pending before the Board to the immigration judge. Parties may, in appropriate circumstances, move to remand proceedings to the immigration judge to consider newly available evidence or newly acquired eligibility for relief.

(b) Requirements — Motions to remand are subject to the same substantive requirements as motions to reopen. See *Matter of Coelho*, 20 I&N Dec. 464 (BIA 1992). Accordingly, evidence and applications for relief, if involved, must be submitted with the motion.

The Board may deny a motion to remand where the evidence was discoverable at an earlier stage in the proceedings, is not material or probative, or is otherwise defective. As with motions to reopen, parties submitting new evidence should articulate the purpose of the new evidence and explain its prior unavailability. See Chapter 5.2(f) (Evidence).

(c) Limitations — Unlike motions to reopen, motions to remand are not limited in time or number because they are made during the pendency of an appeal.

(d) Remands to DHS — Where an appeal is taken from a decision made by a DHS officer, the Board may remand the case to DHS. For example, the Board may remand a visa petition denial to DHS for further development of the petition record. Where an appeal is taken from an immigration judge decision, however, the Board cannot remand proceedings to DHS. For example, the Board cannot remand proceedings to a DHS Asylum Office once an immigration judge has ruled on an asylum application.

(e) Post-Remand Appeals — If the Board grants a motion to remand resulting in a new immigration judge decision, a party may file a new appeal. In that new appeal, the party may pursue any new issues or any unresolved issues from the prior appeal.

5.9   Other Motions

(a) Motion to Expedite — See Chapter 6.4 (Expedite Requests).

(b) Motion to Withdraw Appeal — Motions to withdraw an appeal are discussed in Chapter 4.11 (Withdrawing an Appeal). Parties are reminded not to confuse a motion to withdraw an appeal with a motion to remand. If a party wishes a case returned to the immigration judge for consideration of a newly available form of relief (e.g. adjustment of status), the correct motion is a *motion to remand*. In contrast, when a motion to withdraw an appeal is filed, the decision of the immigration judge immediately becomes final as if no appeal had ever been filed. If an appeal is withdrawn, DHS may remove or deport the respondent, if the immigration judge so ordered. See Chapters 4.11 (Withdrawing an Appeal), 5.8 (Motions to Remand).

(c) Motion to Withdraw as Counsel or Practitioner of Record — See Chapter 2.1(b)(3) (Change in Representation).

(d) Motion to Stay Deportation or Removal — See Chapter 6 (Stays and Expedite Requests).

(e) Motion to Consolidate — See Chapter 4.10 (Combining and Separating Appeals).

(f) Motion to Sever — See Chapter 4.10 (Combining and Separating Appeals).

(g) Motion to Join — See Chapter 4.10 (Combining and Separating Appeals).

(h) Motion to Recalendar — When proceedings have been administratively closed or continued indefinitely and a party wishes to "reopen" those proceedings, the proper motion is a motion to recalendar, *not* a motion to reopen. A motion to recalendar should provide the date and the reason for the case being closed. If available, a copy of the closure order should be attached to the motion. Motions to recalendar should be properly filed, clearly captioned, and comply with the general motion requirements. See Chapter 5.2 (Filing a Motion), Appendix E (Cover Pages). To ensure that the Board has the respondent's current address, a Change of Address Form (EOIR-33/BIA) should also be filed. Motions to recalendar are not subject to time and number restrictions, nor do they require a fee or Fee Waiver Request (Form EOIR-26A).

(i) Motion to Hold in Abeyance — The Board does not normally entertain motions to hold cases in abeyance while other matters are pending (e.g., waiting for a visa petition to become current, waiting for criminal conviction to be overturned).

(j) Motion to Stay Suspension — Motions involving the discipline of a practitioner are discussed in Chapter 11 (Discipline).

(k) Motion to Amend — The Board will entertain a motion to amend a previous filing in limited situations (e.g., to correct a clerical error in a filing). The motion should clearly articulate what needs to be corrected in the previous filing. The filing of a motion to amend does not affect any existing appeal or motion deadlines.

(I) Other Types of Motions — The Board will entertain other types of motions, as appropriate to the facts and law of each particular case, provided that the motion is properly filed, is clearly captioned, and complies with the general motion requirements. See Chapter 5.2 (Filing a Motion), Appendix E (Cover Pages).

5.10 Decisions

Upon the entry of a decision, the Board serves its decision upon the parties by regular mail, or through ECAS in eligible cases. See Chapter 1.4(d) (Board Decisions). A courtesy copy of the Board's decision is also served by regular mail upon a represented respondent.

5.11 Non-Opposition to Motion

A motion will be deemed unopposed unless the opposing party responds within 13 days from the date of service of the motion. See generally 8 C.F.R. § 1003.2(g)(3). However, the opposing party's failure to oppose a motion, or affirmative non-opposition to a motion, will not necessarily result in a grant of that motion. See Chapter 4.12 (Non-Opposition to Appeal).

This page intentionally left blank.

Chapter 6 Stays and Expedite Requests

6.1   In General

A stay prevents DHS from executing an order of removal, deportation, or exclusion. Stays are automatic in some instances and discretionary in others. This chapter provides general guidance regarding the procedures to follow when filing for a stay before the immigration court or the Board. For particular cases, parties should note that the procedures are not the same before the immigration court and the Board and should consult the controlling law and regulations. See INA §§ 240(b)(5)(C), 240(c)(7)(C)(iv); 8 C.F.R. §§ 1003.2(f), 1003.6, 1003.23(b)(1)(v), and 1003.23(b)(4)(ii), (iii)(C).

A respondent under a final order of deportation or removal may seek a stay of deportation or removal from DHS. A denial of the stay by DHS does not preclude an immigration judge or the Board from granting a stay in connection with a previously filed motion to reopen or motion to reconsider. DHS shall take all reasonable steps to comply with a stay granted by an immigration judge or the Board, but such a stay shall cease to have effect if granted or communicated after the respondent has been placed aboard an aircraft or other conveyance for removal and the normal boarding has been completed. 8 C.F.R. §§ 241.6, 1241.6.

In the context of bond proceedings, the Board has the authority to grant a stay of the execution of an immigration judge's decision when DHS has appealed or provided notice of intent to appeal by filing the Notice of Service Intent to Appeal Custody Redetermination (Form EOIR-43) with the immigration court within one business day of the immigration judge's bond order, and file the appeal within 10 business days. The Board may also entertain motions to reconsider discretionary stays it has granted. See 8 C.F.R. § 1003.19(i)(1)-(2); see also Chapter 6.3 (Discretionary Stays).

There are important differences between the automatic stay provisions in deportation and exclusion proceedings and the automatic stay provisions in removal proceedings. Other than a motion to reopen in absentia deportation proceedings, those differences are not covered in this Practice Manual. Accordingly, parties in deportation or exclusion proceedings should carefully review the controlling law and regulations.

6.2   Automatic Stays

There are certain circumstances when an immigration judge's order of removal is automatically stayed pending further action on an appeal or motion. When a stay is automatic, the immigration courts and the Board do not issue a written order on the stay.

(a) During the Appeal Period — After an immigration judge issues a final decision on the merits of a case (not including bond or custody, credible fear, claimed status review, or reasonable fear determinations), the order is automatically stayed for the 30-day period for filing an appeal with the Board. However, the order is not stayed if the losing party waived the right to appeal. 8 C.F.R. § 1003.6(a).

(b) During the Adjudication of an Appeal — If a party appeals an immigration judge's decision on the merits of the case (not including bond and custody determinations) to the Board during the appeal period, the order of removal is automatically stayed during the Board's adjudication of the appeal. 8 C.F.R. § 1003.6(a). The stay remains in effect until the Board renders a final decision in the case.

(c) During the Adjudication of Case Certified to the Board — A removal order is stayed while the Board adjudicates a case that is before that appellate body by certification. 8 C.F.R. § 1003.6(a); see also Chapter 4.18 (Certification by an Immigration Judge). The stay remains in effect until the Board renders a final decision in the case or declines to accept certification of the case.

(d) Motions to Reopen —

(1) Removal proceedings — An immigration judge's removal order is stayed during the period between the filing of a motion to reopen removal proceedings conducted in absentia and the immigration judge's ruling on that motion. 8 C.F.R. § 1003.23(b)(4)(ii). An immigration judge's removal order is automatically stayed during the Board's adjudication of an appeal of the immigration judge's ruling in certain motions to reopen filed by battered spouses, children, and parents. INA § 240(c)(7)(C)(iv). An immigration judge's order is not automatically stayed in appeals to the Board from an immigration judge's denial of a motion to reopen removal proceedings conducted in absentia, and motions to reopen or reconsider a prior Board decision are not automatically stayed.

(2) Deportation proceedings — An immigration judge's deportation order is stayed during the period between the filing of a motion to reopen deportation proceedings conducted in absentia under prior INA § 242B and the immigration judge's ruling on that motion, as well as during the adjudication by the Board of any subsequent appeal of that motion. 8 C.F.R. § 1003.23(b)(4)(iii)(C).

Automatic stays only attach to the original appeal from an immigration judge's denial of a motion to reopen deportation proceedings conducted in absentia under prior INA § 242B. See 8 C.F.R. § 1003.23(b)(4)(iii)(C). Additionally, there is no automatic stay to a motion to reopen or reconsider the Board's prior dismissal of an appeal from an immigration judge's denial of a motion to reopen deportation proceedings conducted in absentia under prior INA § 242B.

(e) Federal Court Remands — A federal court remand to the Board results in an automatic stay of an order of removal if:

- The Board's decision before the federal court involved a direct appeal of an immigration judge's decision on the merits of the case (excluding bond and custody determinations); or

- The Board's decision before the federal court involved an appeal of an immigration judge's denial of a motion to reopen deportation proceedings conducted in absentia under prior INA § 242B.

6.3   Discretionary Stays

(a) Jurisdiction — Both immigration judges and the Board have authority to grant and reconsider stays as a matter of discretion but only for matters within the judges' or the Board's respective jurisdiction. See Chapters 1.4 (Jurisdiction and Authority), 7.2 (Jurisdiction). Immigration judges consider requests for discretionary stays only when a motion to reopen or a motion to reconsider is pending before the immigration court.

In most cases, the Board entertains stays only when there is an appeal from an immigration judge's denial of a motion to reopen removal proceedings or a motion to reopen or reconsider a prior Board decision pending before the Board. The Board may also consider a stay of an immigration judge's bond decision while a bond appeal is pending in order to prevent the respondent's release from detention. See Chapter 7.3(a)(4) (Stays).

(b) Motion to Reopen to Apply for Asylum, Withholding of Removal under the Act, or Protection under the Convention Against Torture — Time and numerical limitations do not apply to motions to reopen to apply for asylum, withholding of removal under the Act, or protection under the Convention Against Torture if the motion is based on changed country conditions arising in the country of nationality or the country to which removal has been ordered, if such evidence is material and was not available and could not have been discovered or presented at the previous proceeding. The filing of a motion to reopen in such circumstances does not automatically stay a respondent's removal. The respondent may request a stay and if granted by the immigration court shall not be removed pending disposition of the motion. If the original asylum application was denied based on a finding that it was frivolous, the respondent is ineligible to file a motion to reopen or reconsider or for a stay of removal. 8 C.F.R. § 1003.23(b)(4)(i).

When filing a motion to reopen to apply for asylum, withholding of removal under the Act, or protection under the Convention Against Torture based on changed country conditions, the respondent does not need to file a copy of their record of proceedings or A file.

(c) Motion Required — Parties should submit a request for a discretionary stay by filing a written motion. The motion should comply with all the requirements for filing, including formatting, inclusion of a proof of service, and submission of possible fees. See Chapter 3 (Filing with the Board), Appendix E (Cover Pages).

(1) Contents — A party requesting a discretionary stay of removal before the immigration court should submit a motion stating the complete case history and all relevant facts. It should also include a copy of the order that the party wants stayed, if available. If the moving party does not have a copy of the order, that party should provide the date of the order and a detailed description of the immigration judge's ruling and reasoning, as articulated by the immigration judge. If the facts are in dispute, the moving party should provide appropriate evidence. A discretionary request to stay removal, deportation, or exclusion may be submitted at any time after a respondent becomes subject to a final order of removal, deportation, or exclusion if a motion to reopen or reconsider is pending before the immigration court.

A party requesting a discretionary stay of removal, deportation, or exclusion before Board should follow the procedures described below:

(A) Who may request — A respondent (or a respondent's practitioner of record) may request a discretionary stay of removal, deportation, or exclusion only if the respondent's case is currently before the Board and the respondent is subject to a removal, deportation, or exclusion order.

(B) Timing of request — A request to stay removal, deportation, or exclusion may be submitted at any time during the pendency of a case before the Board.

(C) Form of request — Requests to stay removal, deportation, or exclusion must be made in writing. The Board prefers that stay requests be submitted in the form of a "MOTION TO STAY REMOVAL." See Appendix E (Cover Pages).

(D) Contents — The motion should contain a complete recitation of the relevant facts and case history and indicate the current status of the case. The motion must also contain a specific statement of the time exigencies involved. Motions containing vague or general statements of urgency are not persuasive.

A copy of the existing immigration judge or Board order should be included, when available. When the moving party does not have a copy of the order, the moving party should provide the date of the immigration judge's decision and a detailed description of both the ruling and the basis of that ruling, as articulated by the immigration judge. If the facts are in dispute, the moving party should furnish evidence supporting the motion to stay.

(E) Format — The motion should comply with the general rules for filing motions. See Chapter 5.2 (Filing a Motion). The motion must include a Proof of Service. See Chapter 3.2 (Service), Appendix F (Cert. of Service).

(F) Fee — A motion to stay removal, deportation, or exclusion does not, by itself, require a filing fee. The underlying appeal or motion, however, may still require a fee. See Chapter 3.4 (Filing Fees).

(2) Emergency v. non-emergency — The immigration courts and the Board categorize stay requests into two categories: emergency and non-emergency. When filing a stay request with the immigration court, the parties should submit their motion with a cover page either labeled "MOTION TO STAY REMOVAL" or "EMERGENCY MOTION TO STAY REMOVAL," as relevant.

(A) Emergency — The immigration courts and the Board may rule immediately on an "emergency" stay request. The immigration court and the Board only consider a stay request to be an emergency when a respondent is:

1. in DHS's physical custody and removal, deportation, or exclusion is imminent;

2. turning themselves in to DHS custody in order to be removed, deported, or excluded and removal, deportation, or exclusion is expected to occur within the next 3 business days; or

3. scheduled to self-execute an order of removal, deportation, or exclusion within the next 3 business days.

The motion should contain a specific statement of the time exigencies involved.

If a party is seeking an emergency stay from the Board, the party must contact the Board's Emergency Stay Unit by calling 703-306-0093. If a party is seeking an emergency stay from an immigration court, they must call the immigration court from which the removal order was issued. EOIR otherwise will not be able to properly process the request as an emergency stay. The Board's Emergency Stay Unit is closed on federal holidays. It will consider an emergency stay request only on non-holiday weekdays from 9:00 a.m. to 5:30 p.m. (Eastern Time). Immigration courts will consider stay requests during posted operating hours.

A respondent may supplement a non-emergency stay request with an emergency stay request if qualifying circumstances, such as when a respondent reports to DHS custody for imminent removal, arise.

Parties can obtain instructions for filing an emergency stay motion with the Board by calling the same numbers. For a list of immigration court numbers, see Appendix A (Directory) in the Immigration Court Practice Manual or visit EOIR's website at www.justice.gov/eoir/eoir-immigration-court-listing.

When circumstances require immediate attention from the Board or immigration courts, EOIR may, at the adjudicator's discretion, entertain a telephonic stay request.

EOIR promptly notifies the parties of its decision.

(B) Non-emergency — The immigration courts and the Board do not rule immediately on a "non-emergency" stay request. Instead, the request is considered during the normal course of adjudication. Non-emergency stay requests include those from respondents who are not facing removal within the next 3 business days, and who are either:

1. not in detention; or

2. in detention but not facing imminent removal, deportation, or exclusion.

(d) Pending Motions — Neither the immigration judges nor the Board automatically grant discretionary stays. The mere filing of a motion for a discretionary stay of an order does not prevent the execution of the order. Therefore, DHS may execute the underlying removal, deportation, or exclusion order unless and until the immigration judge or the Board grants the motion for a stay.

(e) Adjudication and Notice — When an immigration judge or the Board grants a discretionary stay of removal, deportation, or exclusion, the immigration judge or the Board issues a written order. When a discretionary stay is granted, the parties are promptly notified about the decision.

(f) Duration — A discretionary stay of removal, deportation, or exclusion lasts until the immigration judge adjudicates the motion to reopen or motion to reconsider or until the Board renders a final decision on the merits of the appeal, motion to reopen, or the motion to reconsider.

6.4   Expedite Requests

(a) Requirements — Appeals and motions may be expedited only upon the filing of a motion to expedite and a demonstration of impending and irreparable harm or similar good cause. The motion must contain a complete articulation of the reasons to expedite and the consequences to the moving party if the request is not granted.

Expedited requests are generally not favored and should be requested only in compelling circumstances. Examples of appropriate reasons to request expedited treatment include: (i) imminent removal from the United States; (ii) imminent ineligibility for relief, such as a minor "aging out" of derivative status; (iii) circumstances threatening to moot the appeal absent prompt action by the Board; and (iv) a health crisis precipitating a need for immediate Board action.

(b) Procedure — Motions to expedite should be filed in accordance with the general rules and procedures for other motions. See Chapter 5.2 (Filing a Motion). Any request for expeditious processing should be made through a written "MOTION TO EXPEDITE that bears the name and A-number of the affected respondent and articulates the grounds for the request. Use of a cover page is highly recommended. See Appendix E (Cover Pages). In a genuine emergency, a party may contact the Clerk's Office of the Board by telephone. See Appendix A (Directory). Even in such situations, the moving party must be prepared to file a written "MOTION TO EXPEDITE" immediately.

(c) Response — The Board will consider all expedited requests that are properly filed. When a request is granted, the Board will expedite the case without notifying the parties that the request has been granted. For administrative reasons, the Board cannot reply to all requests.

.

This page intentionally left blank.

Chapter 7 Bond

7.1 Bond Appeals Generally

In certain circumstances, a respondent detained by the Department of Homeland Security (DHS) can be released from custody. When a respondent asks an immigration judge to review a DHS custody decision, it is called a "bond redetermination." Appeals from custody decisions are commonly called "bond appeals." Bond proceedings are separate from removal proceedings. See generally 8 C.F.R. §§ 1003.19, 1236.1.

Bond proceedings differ procedurally from other immigration proceedings. For example, a respondent can request a bond redetermination without a formal motion, without paying a fee, and without the usual filing deadlines.

7.2 Jurisdiction

(a) Continuing Jurisdiction — A respondent may ask the immigration judge or DHS to change a bond decision if:

- the respondent is in detention (or was in detention within the last seven days),

- the respondent's removal or deportation proceedings are still open before an immigration judge or the Board, and

- the request for a change in bond is not moot as described in Chapter 7.4 (Mootness)

The respondent may ask even if:

- the respondent has previously asked the immigration judge to change a bond decision, *provided* the respondent can show that their circumstances have changed materially since the last bond decision

- the respondent appealed a previous bond decision to the Board

(b) Appellate Jurisdiction —

(1) Immigration judge decisions — The Board has jurisdiction over appeals of immigration judge bond rulings. See 8 C.F.R. §§ 1003.1(b)(7), 1003.19(f), 1003.38, 1236.1(d)(3)(i). The Board also has general emergency stay authority when DHS appeals an immigration judge's custody decision. See 8 C.F.R. § 1003.19(h)(4)(i).

(2) DHS decisions — The Board has jurisdiction over certain appeals involving DHS bond decisions made subsequent to an immigration judge ruling. See 8 C.F.R. § 1236.1(d)(3). The Board does *not* have jurisdiction over appeals from DHS custody decisions involving:

- respondents in exclusion proceedings

- "arriving aliens," as defined in 8 C.F.R. § 1001.1(q), in removal proceedings

- respondents ineligible for release on security or related grounds

- respondents ineligible for release on certain criminal grounds

8 C.F.R. § 1003.19(h)(2)(i).

(3) Jurisdictional issues — The Board has jurisdiction to rule on whether an immigration judge has jurisdiction to make a bond determination.

(c) No Jurisdiction — The Board does not have authority to review a bond decision when the respondent:

- departs the United States, whether voluntarily or involuntarily

- is granted relief by the immigration judge and DHS does not appeal

- is granted relief from removal by the Board

- is denied relief from removal by the immigration judge and the respondent does not appeal

- is denied relief from removal by the Board

- is released on the conditions requested in the bond appeal

- is released on conditions more favorable than those requested in the bond appeal

- has a subsequent bond redetermination request granted by an immigration judge and DHS does not appeal

7.3   Procedure

(a) Filing — When a respondent may appeal the bond decision of an immigration judge, the appeal is filed in the same manner as any other appeal of an immigration judge decision. See Chapter 3 (Filing with the Board), 4 (Appeals of Immigration Judge Decisions). In those few instances in which a respondent may appeal to the Board from the custody determination of DHS, the appeal is filed in the same manner as a visa petition appeal. See Chapters 7.2(b)(2) (DHS decisions), 9 (Visa Petitions).

(1) Separate Notice of Appeal — A bond appeal must be filed on its own Notice of Appeal (Form EOIR-26, if an immigration judge decision, or Form EOIR-29, if a DHS decision) and *must not* be combined with an appeal of a decision regarding the respondent's removal or deportation (often referred to as the decision "on the merits" of the case). The Notice of Appeal should be completed in full and specify the date of the bond decision being appealed.

(2) Deadline —

(A) Immigration judge decision — When an immigration judge renders the bond decision, the appeal has the same 30-day deadline as any other appeal from an immigration judge decision. See Chapter 4.5 (Appeal Deadlines).

(B) Department of Homeland Security decision — In the limited instances in which the Board has jurisdiction over the appeal from a DHS bond decision, the deadline for filing an appeal is 10 days from the date of the DHS bond decision. See 8 C.F.R. § 1236.1(d)(3). See also Chapter 3.1(b) (Must be "Timely").

(3) Fee — Generally, there is no filing fee for a bond appeal. However, when a respondent is appealing the amount of a voluntary departure bond in removal proceedings, there is a $110 filing fee.

(4) Stays —

(A) Stays of deportation or removal — Stays of deportation or removal are not available in bond proceedings. See 8 C.F.R. § 1236.1(d)(4). See also Chapter 6 (Stays and Expedite Requests).

(B) Stays of bond decisions — If a respondent appeals a bond decision, that decision remains in effect while the appeal is pending. The same is true for a DHS appeal, unless the decision is "stayed" by regulation (which here means that the immigration judge's decision does not go into effect and the DHS decision to detain the respondent remains in effect until the Board decides the appeal). See 8 C.F.R. § 1003.19(i)(2).

A bond decision is stayed by regulation when either:

- DHS has determined that a respondent should not be released, but the immigration judge authorized the respondent's release

- DHS sets a bond of $10,000 or more, but the immigration judge sets a lower bond amount

For such a stay to take effect, DHS must file a Notice of Service Intent to Appeal Custody Redetermination (Form EOIR-43) with the immigration court within one business day of the immigration judge's bond order, and file the appeal within 10 business days. The stay remains in effect until the Board decides the appeal, or 90 days from the filing of the appeal, whichever occurs first. The 90 days is tolled 21 days if the Board grants a respondent's briefing extension request and is extended if a discretionary stay is pending or for referral to the Attorney General.

When a stay is not automatic, DHS may ask the Board to grant an emergency stay. See 8 C.F.R. § 1003.19(i)(1), *Matter of Joseph*, 22 I&N Dec. 660 (BIA 1999). See also Chapter 6 (Stays and Expedited Requests).

(b) Processing — Appeals of bond decisions made by immigration judges are briefed and processed in the same manner as appeals of immigration judge removal decisions, except that bond hearings are not transcribed. See Chapters 3 (Filing with the Board), 4 (Appeals of Immigration Judge Decisions). Appeals of bond decisions made by DHS officers are briefed and processed in the same manner as visa petition appeals. See Chapter 9 (Visa Petitions).

(1) Briefing schedule — Where the appeal is taken from an immigration judge decision, the Board issues a filing receipt and a briefing schedule. See Chapter 4.2(e) (Briefing Schedule). Where the appeal is taken from a DHS decision, DHS is responsible for the briefing schedule. See Chapter 9.3(d)(2) (Briefing schedule). Briefs, when submitted, should comply with the general rules for briefing. See Chapter 4.6 (Appeal Briefs).

(2) Transcripts — Bond proceedings are less formal than other immigration court proceedings. See *Matter of Chirinos*, 16 I&N Dec. 276 (BIA 1977). Bond hearings are seldom recorded and are not routinely transcribed. See generally Chapter 4.2(f) (Transcription).

(3) Decision — Upon entry of a decision regarding a bond appeal, the Board serves the decision on the parties by regular mail, or through ECAS in eligible cases. See Chapter 1.4(d) (Board Decisions). A courtesy copy of the Board's decision is also served by regular mail upon a represented respondent.

7.4   Mootness

A bond appeal is deemed moot whenever the respondent:

- departs the United States, whether voluntarily or involuntarily

- is granted relief by the immigration judge and the DHS does not appeal

- is granted relief by the Board

- is denied relief by the immigration judge and the respondent does not appeal

- is denied relief by the Board

- is released on the conditions requested in the appeal

Chapter 8 Oral Argument

8.1   Oral Argument Coordinator

All inquiries and requests (not coming from the news media) regarding the scheduling, attendance, seating, and administration of oral argument should be directed to the Oral Argument Coordinator. News media should contact the Office of Communications and Legislative Affairs. See Chapter 8.5(c) (News Media).

All correspondence must be addressed as follows:

Oral Argument Coordinator
Clerk's Office
Board of Immigration Appeals
5107 Leesburg Pike, Suite 2000
Falls Church, Virginia 22041

The Oral Argument Coordinator may also be reached at (703) 605-1007.

8.2   Selection of Cases

(a) Appeals — Oral argument is held at the discretion of the Board and is rarely granted. When an appeal has been taken, oral argument, if desired, must be requested on the Notice of Appeal. 8 C.F.R. § 1003.1(e)(7). Oral argument must be requested at the outset of the appeal, or oral argument may be deemed waived. In either the Notice of Appeal or a brief, the appealing party should explain the reason for requesting oral argument and articulate how oral argument would supplement any written submissions. The Board generally does not seek oral argument from parties who do not request it.

(b) Motions — Oral argument is available, though infrequently granted, to parties moving to have the Board reopen or reconsider their case. 8 C.F.R. § 1003.2(h). The moving party should request oral argument in a separate but accompanying document with a cover page labeled "REQUEST FOR ORAL ARGUMENT." See Appendix E (Cover Pages). The request must explain the reason for requesting oral argument and articulate how oral argument would supplement any written submissions. While the Board reserves the authority to schedule oral argument, the Board generally does not seek oral argument from parties who did not initially request it.

(c) Requests by Responding Parties — Either party to an appeal or motion may request oral argument.

(1) Appeals — In the event the party opposing the appeal wishes to request oral argument, the request must be made prior to the expiration of the briefing schedule. That party should request oral argument in a separate but accompanying document with a cover page labeled "REQUEST FOR ORAL ARGUMENT." See Appendix E (Cover Pages). The request must explain the reason for requesting oral argument and articulate how oral argument would supplement any written submissions.

(2) Motions — In the event that a party responding to a motion wishes to request oral argument, the request should accompany the reply to the motion, which itself must be filed in accordance with the deadline set in the regulations. See 8 C.F.R. § 1003.2(g)(3). That party should request oral argument in a separate but accompanying document with a cover page labeled "REQUEST FOR ORAL ARGUMENT." See Appendix E (Cover Pages). The request must explain the reason for requesting oral argument and articulate how oral argument would supplement any written submissions.

(d) Criteria — Cases are selected for oral argument because they meet one or more of a number of criteria, including but not limited to: (i) the resolution of an issue of first impression; (ii) alteration, modification, or clarification of an existing rule of law; (iii) reaffirmation of an existing rule of law; (iv) the resolution of a conflict of authority; and (v) discussion of an issue of significant public interest.

8.3   Notification

(a) Request Granted — If a request for oral argument is granted, the Board notifies the parties through a notice of selection sent after the briefing schedule has concluded. The notice will specify the time and place scheduled for oral arguments, and the issues the parties need to address. Parties are generally provided at least 30 days' advance notice of the date scheduled for oral argument. The parties are also provided with a copy of this chapter, and any other materials the Board deems appropriate.

(1) Confirmation received — Once a party confirms interest in oral argument, the oral argument calendar is fixed, and the parties are subject to the rules and obligations that attach to oral argument. Supplemental briefs may be filed, but the parties are not sent a supplemental briefing schedule. See Chapter 8.7(d)(5) (Supplemental briefs).

(2) Confirmation not received — If a party does not confirm an interest in oral argument, the Board deems the party's request waived and adjudicates the case on the existing record.

(3) Continuance or postponement — Parties are expected to make all reasonable efforts to resolve conflicts in their schedules to permit them to attend oral argument as scheduled. In view of the difficulty in meeting the scheduling needs of the Board and the parties, the Board disfavors motions for continuance or postponement.

(b) Request Denied — If a request for oral argument is denied, the Board does not specifically notify the parties but simply adjudicates the merits of the appeal or motion. Thus, parties should never assume that oral argument will be granted. The Board's Oral Argument Coordinator will notify the parties when a request for oral argument has been granted.

8.4   Location

Oral argument is conducted on site at the Board in Falls Church, Virginia. In rare instances, the Board may conduct oral argument in a location other than Falls Church. 8 C.F.R. § 1003.1(e)(7).

Due to the outbreak of COVID-19, the Board is also authorized to conduct oral argument by telephone or by video teleconferencing.

8.5 Public Access

(a) General Public —

(1) Oral argument — With the exceptions noted below, oral argument is generally open to the public and employees of the Department of Justice, subject to space limitations and priorities given to the parties and the news media. See generally 8 C.F.R. § 1003.27(a).

- Oral arguments involving applications for asylum or withholding of deportation/removal, or a claim brought under the Convention Against Torture are open to the public *unless* the respondent (or the respondent's practitioner of record, if represented) expressly requests that the oral argument be closed. In cases involving such applications or claims, the Board will inquire of the respondent (or the respondent's practitioner of record) whether the oral argument should be closed.

- Exclusion proceedings are closed to the public *unless* respondent (or the respondent's practitioner of record, if represented) expressly requests that the oral argument be open to the public.

- Oral arguments involving a respondent abused spouse or child are closed to the public. Oral arguments involving a respondent spouse may be open to the public if the abused spouse expressly agrees that the oral argument and record of proceedings will be open to the public.

- Oral arguments are closed to the public if information is to be presented or discussed which is subject to a protective order or documents filed under seal by DHS.

See generally 8 C.F.R. §§ 1003.27, 1003.31(d), 1003.46, 1208.6, 1240.10(b), 1240.11(c)(3)(i), 1240.32, 1240.33(c)(1). Only parties, their practitioners of record, and persons authorized by the Board in advance, including employees of the Department of Justice, may attend a closed argument. If classified information is to be presented, or discussed during an oral argument, the proceedings are closed to the public. Also, no one may be present in the oral argument room without, among other things, the appropriate security clearance and a legitimate "need-to-know" the information. See generally Executive Order 13526 and any related orders.

The Board may limit attendance or hold a closed hearing if appropriate to protect parties or witnesses, or when a closed hearing is otherwise in the public interest. See generally 8 C.F.R. § 1003.27(b).

(2) Requests to open oral argument — In appropriate cases, parties may waive their right to a closed hearing and permit oral argument to be open to the public. The request must be made in writing and sent to the Oral Argument Coordinator at least 15 days prior to the scheduled date of oral argument. The request must be served upon the other party. See Chapter 3.2 (Service). The request should be phrased as follows:

"I hereby request and consent that oral argument in the matter of [name of party] be open to the public and, further, I hereby consent that information contained within the record of proceedings may be released to the public. I acknowledge that this waiver of confidentiality may not be withdrawn after oral argument has begun."

Parties may not retract their request within 24 hours of the scheduled time for oral argument. Also, parties may not request that specific persons be excluded from an open oral argument.

(3) Requests to close oral argument — Certain types of oral argument cases are automatically closed to the public. See Chapter 8.5(a)(1) (Oral argument). The Board may, at its discretion, close oral argument. See generally 8 C.F.R. § 1003.27(b). A party may request that oral argument be closed but must do so in writing at least 15 days prior to the time of oral argument and serve the request on the other party. See Chapter 3.2 (Service). The request must set forth in detail the rationale for closing the hearing.

(4) Reserved seating — A party may request that the Board reserve up to 5 gallery seats for the party's invitees. A reserved seating request must be made to the Oral Argument Coordinator at least 15 days prior to the scheduled date of oral argument. The Board tries to accommodate all reasonable requests for additional seating, subject to space limitations and any special considerations that may arise.

(b) Recording and Broadcasting — The public, including the parties and the news media, may not bring any recording or broadcasting devices into oral argument, whether photographic, audio, video, or electronic in nature. See generally 8 C.F.R. § 1003.28.

(c) News Media — Representatives of the news media may attend oral argument that is open to the public. The Board reserves 10 gallery seats for members of the media. The news media are subject to the general prohibition on recording and broadcasting. See subsection (b), above. The news media are welcome to contact the Communications and Legislative Affairs Division for information about cases selected for oral argument and to request reserved seating. Seating reservations should be made at least 24 hours in advance of the scheduled time for oral argument. See Appendix A (Directory).

8.6   Appearances

(a) Notices of Appearance — Only parties, their practitioners of record, and amicus curiae invited by the Board may participate in oral argument. See generally Chapter 2.1 (Representation and Appearances Generally). Every practitioner who wishes to argue before the Board must file a Notice of Entry of Appearance as

Attorney or Representative Before the Board of Immigration Appeals (Form EOIR-27). See Chapter 2.1(b) (Entering an Appearance as the Practitioner of Record). If, at any time after the filing of the appeal, there is a change in representation, the new practitioner must immediately file a Form EOIR-27. See Chapters 2.1(b) (Entering an Appearance as the Practitioner of Record), 2.1(b)(3) (Change in Representation).

(b) Multiple Practitioners — Parties are limited to one practitioner of record to present oral argument. See Chapter 2.1(b)(4) (Multiple practitioners of record). If a practitioner of record wishes to share oral argument with another practitioner, or wishes another practitioner to argue in their place, they must submit a written request to the Oral Argument Coordinator at least 15 days in advance of the scheduled oral argument. The request must also be served upon the other party. That practitioner must both satisfy the appearance requirements and file a separate Notice of Appearance (Form EOIR-27). See Chapter 2.1 (Representation and Appearances Generally). The Form EOIR-27 should reflect that their appearance is solely for the purpose of participating in oral argument, which is done by writing in large letters at the top of the form the words: "ORAL ARGUMENT ONLY." A paper copy of the Form EOIR-27 must be sent directly to the Oral Argument Coordinator.

Practitioners who appear solely for the purpose of oral argument are advised that, once oral argument is concluded, all notices and Board correspondence will be sent only to the practitioner of record. The practitioner of record is responsible for providing copies of notices or correspondence to the practitioner who entered an appearance strictly for oral argument purposes.

(c) Motions to Withdraw — Once oral argument is scheduled, motions to withdraw as counsel are entertained only where good cause is shown. See Chapter 2.1(b)(3)(C) (Withdrawal of counsel). Substitution of counsel is permitted. See Chapter 2.3(b)(3)(A) (Substitution of counsel).

8.7   Rules of Oral Argument

(a) Attire — The Board expects all persons to respect the decorum of the court. Practitioners are expected to appear in business attire. All others in attendance are expected to dress in proper attire.

(b) Electronic Devices —

(1) Recording devices — Only the Board may record oral argument. No devices of any kind, including cameras, video recorders, and cassette/digital recorders, may be used by any person other than the Board to record any part of the oral argument.

(2) Possession of electronic devices during oral argument — Subject to section (3) below, all persons - including parties and members of the press - may bring laptop computers, tablets, cellular telephones, electronic calendars, and other electronic devices commonly used to conduct business activities, including electronic devices which have collateral recording capability provided that they are *not* used to record the oral argument. All electronic devices must be turned off in courtrooms and during oral argument, unless otherwise authorized under section (3) below. Outside of courtrooms and oral argument, electronic devices may be used in non-recording mode, but they must be made silent, and usage must be limited and non-disruptive. For further discussion on the use of electronic devices, see EOIR PM 19-10, *EOIR Security Directive: Policy for Public Use of Electronic Devices in EOIR Space* (Mar. 20, 2019), available at https://www.justice.gov/eoir/file/1146191/download.

(3) Use of electronic devices during oral argument — Only practitioners of record and attorneys from DHS representing the government may use laptop computers, tablets, electronic calendars, and other electronic devices commonly used to conduct business activities, provided they are used for immediately relevant court and business related activities and *not* used to record the oral argument. Such devices may only be used in silent/vibrate mode. The use of such devices must not disrupt oral argument, and Board Members have the discretion to prohibit the continued use of any electronic devices that pose a disruption to ongoing proceedings. Cellular telephones and other electronic devices must be turned off when not in use to conduct business activities in the courtroom. For further discussion on the use of electronic devices, see EOIR PM 19-10, *EOIR Security Directive: Policy for Public Use of Electronic Devices in EOIR Space* (Mar. 20, 2019), available at https://www.justice.gov/eoir/file/1146191/download.

(c) Conduct — All persons attending oral argument must respect the dignity of the proceedings. Talking is not permitted in the gallery during oral argument, nor may attendees depart or enter the room once oral argument has begun. Disruptive behavior is not tolerated.

(1) Practitioners — Practitioners are expected to observe the professional conduct rules and regulations applicable to EOIR practitioners and of their licensing authorities and to present, at all times, a professional demeanor becoming of an officer of the court.

(2) Represented parties — Parties who are represented are welcome, but not required, to attend oral argument. Represented parties are permitted to observe but may not speak during oral argument.

(3) Detained respondents — Detained respondents are not permitted to attend oral argument.

(4) Amici curiae — Amici curiae are subject to the same rules of conduct as practitioners of record. See Chapter 8.7(e)(13) (Amicus curiae).

(d) Prior to Oral Argument —

(1) Check in — On the day of oral argument, parties are required to check in at least 30 minutes prior to the scheduled time for oral argument. The Oral Argument Coordinator will advise the parties regarding the procedures for check in.

(2) Adverse weather conditions — In the event of adverse weather conditions, parties should contact the Oral Argument Coordinator for guidance or otherwise comply with the instructions provided in the selection notice.

(3) Failure to appear for oral argument — In the event that either party fails to appear for oral argument, the Board may hear the argument of the side that does appear, in which case the argument is entered into the record and considered by the Board in rendering its decision. Given the administrative burden of scheduling oral argument, the Board considers an unexplained failure to appear to be a serious discourtesy to both the Board and the other party and will sanction practitioners accordingly. The party whose practitioner fails to appear will not be penalized for that failure, except insofar as that party will be deprived of the benefit of their case being argued.

(4) Late arrival for oral argument — If a party is unable to arrive for oral argument at the appointed time due to extenuating circumstances, such as travel delays, the party should immediately contact the Oral Argument Coordinator or, if the Oral Argument Coordinator is not available, a senior manager in the Clerk's Office. See Appendix A (Directory).

(5) Supplemental briefs — While the Board generally does not accept supplemental briefs, an exception is made for cases that have been granted oral argument. Parties may submit supplemental briefs in anticipation of oral argument, but parties are not sent a supplementary briefing schedule. Parties may submit supplemental briefs until 15 days prior to the date of oral argument. Parties may reply to supplemental briefs up until 7 days prior to the date of oral argument. Supplemental briefs should be directed to the Oral Argument Coordinator. Supplemental briefs are subject to the same requirements as other briefs. See generally Chapters 3 (Filing with the Board), 3.2 (Service), 4.6 (Appeal Briefs), 5.4 (Motion Briefs). Amicus curiae are subject to the same supplemental briefing rules and limitations as the parties. See generally Chapters 2.10 (Amicus Curiae), Chapter 4.6(i) (Amicus Curiae Briefs). Supplemental briefs must be served on the opposing party as expeditiously as they are served on the Board.

(6) Additional authorities — Both oral argument and any supplemental briefs should be based on a thorough research of legal authorities and should include all legal authority that a party might wish to rely upon in oral argument. In the event that a party locates additional legal authority subsequent to the filing of a supplemental brief, parties should observe the following:

(A) Supplemental authorities — If a party inadvertently omits a legal authority and wishes to refer to it at oral argument, that party must so notify the Board (and provide a copy, where appropriate) in advance of oral argument. See Chapter 3.2 (Service). Opposing parties must be informed (and provided a copy, where appropriate) as expeditiously as the Board. Parties may not use supplemental authority, however, as an excuse to file a supplemental brief after the time for briefing has expired. Once the supplemental briefing deadline has passed, see subsection (5), above, the Board will not consider any filing that appears in form or substance to be a brief.

(B) New authorities — If a party discovers a newly available authority, that party should inform the Oral Argument Coordinator and the opposing party immediately. Parties should promptly submit a statement regarding the significance, or lack thereof, of the new authority to the matter being argued. The Board will thereafter determine what action, if any, will be taken in light of the new authority.

(7) Exhibits — The Board accepts no new evidence on appeal. If a party wishes to display exhibits used in the proceeding below or wishes to use presentation aids that do not constitute evidence, the party must make prior arrangements with the Oral Argument Coordinator for delivery and display. The party is also responsible for removing any exhibits or presentation aids at the conclusion of the proceeding.

(8) Reviewing the record of proceedings — Parties wishing to review the record of proceedings should make arrangements with the Oral Argument Coordinator prior to oral argument. Absent special arrangements, the record is not available for review in the 2 hours prior to the scheduled time for oral argument.

(e) Oral Argument — Oral argument should be approached as an opportunity to expand upon, and not merely repeat, a party's written arguments. The Board does not accept new evidence on appeal, and the Board also does not hear testimony. Parties arguing before the Board should follow the rules and guidelines below.

(1) Oral argument table — Parties are generally limited to two legal staff each at the oral argument table. This limit includes practitioners, paralegals, and all other personnel. Represented parties who attend oral argument may not sit at the oral argument tables but are provided priority seating in the gallery.

(2) Addressing the Board — Individual Board Members are to be referred to as either "Appellate Immigration Judge _____" or "Board Member _____" or "Your Honor." Titles, such as "Chief Appellate Immigration Judge _____" or "Chairman _____" and "Deputy Chief Appellate Immigration Judge _____" or "Vice Chairman _____," may also be used. The Board Members as a group may be referred to either as "the Board" or "Your Honors."

(3) Standing and sitting — Parties should stand when addressing the Board. A podium is provided, and the parties must speak from that podium during opening and closing statements. At other times, parties may respond to the Board's questions from the oral argument table.

(4) Familiarity with the record — Parties are expected to be thoroughly familiar with the record. Parties should prepare oral argument with the understanding that the Board Members have studied the briefs and are also thoroughly familiar with the record.

(5) Opening statements — At the commencement of oral argument, persons to argue before the Board should rise and introduce themselves. Opening statements are encouraged. An opening statement should include a brief introduction to the case and the core issue or issues being argued. Parties should not read at length from briefs, authorities, or the record.

(6) Recitation of facts — A brief chronological statement of the pertinent facts, where warranted, is welcome at the outset of oral argument. Extensive recitation of facts, however, is discouraged.

(7) Recitation of law — Oral argument should focus upon the critical points of law that can be properly addressed during the time for oral argument. In their oral presentation, parties may not cite to any case, reported or otherwise, that does not appear in either of the parties' briefs, unless one of two conditions is met: the Board and opposing counsel have been notified in advance of the intention to cite to that case, or the citation is in response to a Board Member's question or the opposing party's oral argument. See Chapter 8.7(d)(6) (Additional authorities).

(8) Argument — Parties are generally allotted 30 minutes per side to present their arguments with a portion of time reserved for rebuttal, if desired by a party. If a party anticipates needing more than 30 minutes, the party should submit a request for additional time, in writing, to the Oral Argument Coordinator at least 15 days prior to the date of oral argument. A copy of the request should be served on the opposing party as well.

If oral argument will be shared by two practitioners, the Oral Argument Coordinator must be notified in writing at least 15 days prior to the scheduled oral argument. The allotted time may be apportioned between them according to their discretion. Practitioners should not duplicate each other's arguments.

(9) Rebuttal — At the outset of oral argument or at the conclusion of their presentation, a party may reserve time for rebuttal, provided there is time remaining.

(10) Questions from the bench — Board members may ask questions at any time during oral argument. Parties should answer the Board's questions as directly as possible. Board Member questions apply toward the 30 minutes allotted for argument and do not extend that time.

(11) Marking of time — Parties are notified when their time for oral argument has elapsed. Parties are expected to monitor their own time, especially when reserving time for co-counsel or rebuttal. In the event of disagreement, the Board's timekeeping is controlling.

(12) Cessation of oral argument — At any point during oral argument, the Board may terminate oral argument if further argument appears unnecessary. The Board may terminate oral argument even if a party's allotted time has not expired.

(13) Amicus curiae — Amicus curiae may present oral argument only upon advance permission of the Board. Such permission is granted sparingly. The time allotted to amicus curiae is determined on a case-by-case basis. Amicus curiae argue after both sides have concluded their arguments. Amicus curiae are subject to the same oral argument rules and limitations as the parties.

Where appropriate, the Board may provide parties an opportunity to respond to the oral argument of amicus curiae.

8.8   Conclusion to Oral Argument

(a) Decision of the Board — Decisions are normally not rendered on the day of oral argument. Subsequent to oral argument, cases are processed in the standard manner. See Chapter 1.4(d) (Board Decisions).

(b) Supplemental Briefs — The Board expects all issues to be fully briefed and argued by the conclusion of oral argument. Parties may not file supplemental briefs after oral argument unless they are expressly solicited by the Board or warranted by emergent developments in the law or the case.

(c) Transcripts — The Board digitally records oral argument. A transcript is prepared following oral argument and is served on the parties.

Chapter 9 Visa Petitions

9.1 Visa Petitions Generally

A visa petition is the first step toward obtaining lawful permanent residence for a foreign-born individual or family. It is usually filed by a United States citizen, lawful permanent resident, or employer. Visa petitions are adjudicated by DHS and once approved, may be revoked or revalidated by DHS under certain circumstances. If a visa petition is denied or revoked, or the revalidation of a visa petition is denied, an appeal may be taken to the Board in some instances.

For visa petition appeals within the Board's jurisdiction, DHS is initially responsible for management of the appeal, including the processing of briefs. The Board's role in the appeal process does not begin until the completed record is received from DHS. See 8 C.F.R. § 1003.5(b).

9.2 Jurisdiction Generally

Visa petitions are adjudicated by the appropriate District Director or Service Center Director of the DHS office having jurisdiction over the petition. Upon adjudication of a visa petition, revocation of a visa petition approval, or revalidation of a visa petition approval, the District Director or Service Center Director will notify the petitioner in writing of the decision. An appeal may be taken to the Board where authorized by statute and regulation. See 8 C.F.R. §§ 1003.1(b)(5), 1205.2(d). See also Chapter 1.4 (Jurisdiction and Authority).

9.3 Visa Petition Denials

(a) Jurisdiction — The Board has appellate jurisdiction over family-based immigrant petitions filed in accordance with section 204 of the Immigration and Nationality Act, with the exception of petitions on behalf of certain orphans. See 8 C.F.R. § 1003.1(b)(5). See generally Chapter 1.4 (Jurisdiction and Authority). The Board does not have jurisdiction over employment-based visa petitions. See 8 C.F.R. §§ 103.2, 103.3, 1205.2(d). See also Chapters 1.2(g) (Relationship to the Administrative Appeals Office (AAO)), 1.4 (Jurisdiction and Authority).

(b) Standing — Only the petitioner, not the beneficiary or a third party, may appeal the denial of a visa petition. *Matter of Sano*, 19 I&N Dec. 299 (BIA 1985). Self-petitioners – including battered spouses, battered children, and certain relatives of deceased citizens – also have standing to appeal. See Immigration and Nationality Act §§ 204(a)(1)(A)(ii), (iii), (iv); 204(a)(1)(B)(ii), (iii); and 204(l); 8 C.F.R. § 204.2.

(c) Filing the Appeal —

(1) How to file — Appeals of all visa petition decisions are made on the Notice of Appeal to the Board of Immigration Appeals from a Decision of a DHS Officer (Form EOIR-29). 8 C.F.R. § 1003.3(a)(2). (This form is different from the Form EOIR-26 used in immigration court proceedings.) This form is also used for petition-based appeals from the decisions of Service Center Directors. The appeal form must be signed by the petitioner, not the beneficiary. The rare

exceptions to that rule are those cases in which the individual "self-petitions," such as battered spouses and children, certain widows and widowers, and applicants seeking temporary admission despite being inadmissible (section 212(d)(3)(A) waiver).

(2) Where to file — Unlike appeals from the decisions of immigration judges, appeals of visa petition denials are filed directly with DHS, in accordance with the applicable regulations, any instructions that appear on the DHS decision, and any instructions that appear on the reverse of the Notice of Appeal (Form EOIR-29). See generally 8 C.F.R. § 1003.3(a)(2). The appeal must be filed with the DHS office having administrative control over the petition record.

(3) When to file — The deadline for the appeal is 30 days from the date of service of the decision being appealed.

(4) Fee — The filing fee for a petition-based appeal is $110. See 8 C.F.R. § 1003.8(b). Unlike appeals of immigration judge decisions, the fee for a petition-based appeal is filed directly with DHS, in accordance with DHS instructions. The fee should be paid in the manner instructed by DHS.

(5) Representation — A petitioner may be represented by a practitioner of record through the filing of a Notice of Appearance (Form EOIR-27). See generally Chapter 2.1(b) (Entering an Appearance as the Practitioner of Record). The practitioner should file the Form EOIR-27 directly with DHS, together with the Notice of Appeal (Form EOIR-29). See 8 C.F.R. § 1292.4(a). Until the Board confirms that it has received the petition record from DHS, as discussed in subsection (d) below, practitioners must submit the Form EOIR-27 directly with DHS and should not submit a Form EOIR-27 directly with the Board. Any Form EOIR-27 received prior to the Board receiving the petition record will not be recognized and will not be forwarded to DHS for inclusion in the petition record. Note that the Form EOIR-27 is not the one used to appear before DHS (Notice of Entry of Appearance as Attorney or Accredited Representative (Form G-28)) and that the Board will not recognize a practitioner using Form G-28.

Practitioners are not permitted to make a limited appearance for document assistance through the Notice of Limited Appearance (Form EOIR-60) in cases involving visa petitions adjudicated before the Board. Any Form EOIR-60 and the associated assisted documents will not be recognized and will be rejected. Practitioners who provide document assistance in such cases must file a Notice of Appearance (Form EOIR-27) as discussed above. See Chapter 2.1(c)(3) (Limited Appearances for Document Assistance Only Permitted in Cases that Originated in the Immigration Court).

(6) Supporting briefs — Briefs, if desired, are filed with DHS, at the same office as the Notice of Appeal (Form EOIR-29) and in accordance with any briefing schedule set by DHS. See 8 C.F.R. § 1003.3(c)(2). Requests to extend the time for filing a brief should be directed to DHS. In rare instances, the Board may, in its discretion, authorize briefs to be filed directly with the Board. 8 C.F.R. § 1003.3(c)(2).

Absent special instructions from DHS, briefs on visa petition appeals should generally follow the guidelines set forth in Chapters 3.3 (Documents) and 4.6 (Appeal Briefs).

(7) Evidence — The Board does not consider new evidence on appeal. If new evidence is submitted in the course of an appeal, the submission may be deemed a motion to remand the petition to DHS for consideration of that new evidence. If the petitioner wishes to submit new evidence, the petitioner should articulate the purpose of the new evidence and explain its prior unavailability. Any document submitted to the Board should comport with the guidelines set forth in Chapter 3.3 (Documents).

However, the Board will generally not consider evidence – or remand the petition – where the proffered evidence was expressly requested by DHS and the petitioner was given a reasonable opportunity to provide it before the petition was adjudicated by DHS. See *Matter of Soriano*, 19 I&N Dec. 764 (BIA 1988).

(8) Stipulations — The Board encourages the parties, whenever possible, to stipulate to any facts or events that pertain to the adjudication of the visa petition.

(9) Electronic filing unavailable — Visa petitions are not available for electronic filing through ECAS. Accordingly, all documents related to a visa petition must be submitted as a paper filing.

(d) Processing — Once an appeal has been properly filed with DHS and the petition record is complete, DHS forwards the petition record to the Board for adjudication of the appeal. After the Board receives the record from DHS, the Board issues a notice to the parties acknowledging it has the record and the appeal.

(1) Record on appeal — The record on appeal consists of all decisions and documents in the petition record, including some or all of the following items: visa petition and supporting documentation, DHS notices, evidence submitted in response to DHS notices, DHS decisions, the Notice of Appeal, any briefs on appeal, the record of any prior DHS action, and the record of any prior Board action.

(2) Briefing schedule — Briefing schedules, if any, are issued by DHS and are to be completed prior to the forwarding of the record to the Board. Accordingly, the Board generally does not issue briefing schedules in visa petition cases. See Chapter 9.3(c)(6) (Supporting briefs).

(3) Status inquiries/DHS — Until the record is received by the Board, all status inquiries must be directed to the DHS office where the appeal was filed. *The Board has no record of the appeal until the record is received by the Board.* Since the Board and DHS are distinct and separate entities, the Board cannot track or provide information on cases that remain within the possession of DHS.

(4) Status inquiries/Board — Confirmation that the Board has received a petition record from DHS can be obtained from the Clerk's Office. See Appendix

A (Directory). The Board tracks petition-based appeals by the beneficiary's name and A-number. All status inquiries must contain this information. See generally Chapter 1.6(a) (All Communications).

      (5) Adjudication — Upon the entry of a decision, the Board serves the decision upon the parties by regular mail. An order issued by the Board is final, unless and until it is stayed, modified, rescinded, or overruled by the Board, the Attorney General, or a federal court. An order is deemed effective as of its issuance date unless the order provides otherwise. See Chapter 1.4(d) (Board Decisions).

(e) Motions — Motions filed during the pendency of an appeal should be filed where the record is located. Motions may not be filed with the Board until the petition and record have been received by the Board. See Chapter 9.3(d)(4) (Status inquiries/Board).

All motions filed subsequent to the Board's adjudication of an appeal, including motions to reopen and motions to reconsider the Board's decision are to be filed with the DHS office having administrative control over the record, not with the Board. 8 C.F.R. § 1003.2(g)(2)(ii).

      (f) Withdrawal of Appeal — The petitioner may, at any time prior to the entry of a decision by the Board, voluntarily withdraw the appeal. To withdraw an appeal, the petitioner should file a written request, with a cover page labeled "WITHDRAWAL OF VISA PETITION APPEAL" with either DHS or the Board, whichever holds the file at the time the withdrawal is submitted. See Chapter 4.11 (Withdrawing an Appeal), Appendix E (Cover Pages).

9.4   Visa Revocation Appeals

      (a) Jurisdiction — The Board has appellate jurisdiction over the revocation of visa petition approvals. 8 C.F.R. §§ 1003.1(b)(5), 1205.2(d). The Board does not have jurisdiction over automatic revocations of visa petitions. 8 C.F.R. § 1205.1. See *Matter of Zaidan*, 19 I&N Dec. 297 (BIA 1985).

      (b) Standing — Only the petitioner, not the beneficiary or a third party, may appeal the revocation of a visa petition approval. *Matter of Sano*, 19 I&N Dec. 299 (BIA 1985). Self-petitioners – including battered spouses, battered children, and certain relatives of deceased citizens – also have standing to appeal. 8 C.F.R. § 1205.2(d).

      (c) Filing the Appeal — Revocation appeals are filed according to the same rules as appeals of visa petition denials. See Chapter 9.3(c) (Filing the Appeal). The only difference is that the petitioner or self-petitioner must file the appeal within 15 days after the service of notice of the revocation. 8 C.F.R. § 1205.2(d).

      (d) Processing — Revocation appeals are processed in the same manner as visa petition denials. See Chapter 9.3(d) (Processing).

      (e) Motions — Motions related to revocation appeals are handled in the same manner as motions for visa petition denials. See Chapter 9.3(e) (Motions).

(f) Withdrawal of Appeal — Withdrawals of revocation appeals are handled in the same manner as withdrawals of visa petition appeals. See Chapter 9.3(f) (Withdrawal of Appeal).

9.5   Visa Revalidation Appeals

(a) Jurisdiction — Certain immigrant petitions are valid for a limited period of time, after which they expire unless revalidated. 8 C.F.R. § 214.2(k)(5). The Board has appellate jurisdiction over the revalidation of visa petitions that fall within the Board's jurisdiction. See Chapter 9.2 (Jurisdiction Generally). See also 8 C.F.R. § 1003.1(b)(5).

(b) Standing — Only the petitioner, not the beneficiary or a third party, may appeal a visa petition revalidation decision. *Matter of Sano*, 19 I&N Dec. 299 (BIA 1985).

(c) Filing the Appeal — Appeals of visa revalidation decisions are filed in the same manner as appeals of visa petition denials. See Chapter 9.3(c) (Filing the Appeal).

(d) Processing — Revalidation appeals are processed in the same manner as visa petition denials. See Chapter 9.3(d) (Processing).

(e) Motions — Motions related to revalidation appeals are handled in the same manner as motions for visa petition denials. See Chapter 9.3(e) (Motions).

(f) Withdrawal of Appeal — Withdrawals of revalidation appeals are handled in the same manner as withdrawals of visa petition appeals. See Chapter 9.3(f) (Withdrawal of Appeal).

9.6   Federal Court Remands

(a) Generally — When Board decisions involving visa petitions are reviewed by a federal court, DHS provides that court with a certified copy of the record. Also, since the Board is not a party before the federal courts, the United States government is represented by the Office of Immigration Litigation (OIL) or the United States Attorney's Office. See Chapter 1.2(h) (Relationship to the Office of Immigration Litigation (OIL)). When a federal court remands a case back to the Board for further action, the Board is notified by the office representing the government in the proceedings before the federal court.

The Board cannot advise petitioners or self-petitioners regarding the propriety of or means for seeking judicial review of Board decisions involving visa petitions.

(b) Processing — When the Board receives notification of a federal court's order from the Office of Immigration Litigation (OIL) or the United States Attorney's Office, a written notification is sent to the parties. The Board will obtain the record of proceedings from DHS. In appropriate cases, a briefing schedule is provided to both parties.

(c) Representation — A petitioner may be represented by a practitioner of record through the filing of a Notice of Appearance (Form EOIR-27). See generally Chapter 2.1(b) (Entering an Appearance as the Practitioner of Record). Until the Board confirms that it has received the petition record from DHS, as discussed in subsection (b) above, practitioners must not submit a Form EOIR-27 directly with the Board. Any Form EOIR-27 received prior to the Board receiving the petition record will not be recognized and will not be forwarded to DHS for inclusion in the petition record. Note that the Form EOIR-27 is not the one used to appear before DHS (Notice of Entry of Appearance as Attorney or Accredited Representative (Form G-28)) and that the Board will not recognize a representative using Form G-28.

Practitioners are not permitted to make a limited appearance for document assistance through the Notice of Limited Appearance (Form EOIR-60) in cases involving visa petitions adjudicated before the Board. Any Notice of Limited Appearance (Form EOIR-60) and the associated assisted documents will not be recognized and will be rejected. Practitioners who provide document assistance in such cases must file a Notice of Appearance (Form EOIR-27) as discussed above. See Chapter 2.1(c)(3) (Limited Appearances for Document Assistance Only Permitted in Cases that Originated in the Immigration Court).

Chapter 10 Fines

10.1   Fines Generally

Certain provisions of the Immigration and Nationality Act render individuals and carriers liable for transporting unauthorized respondents into the United States. See Immigration and Nationality Act § 273; 8 C.F.R. part 1280. Fines may be assessed by a DHS Special Agent in Charge, the DHS Associate Director for Operations, U.S. Citizenship and Immigration Services, or the DHS National Fines Office. 8 C.F.R. § 1280.1.

In fines cases, DHS is initially responsible for appeal management, including initial briefing. The Board's role in the appeal process does not begin until the completed record is received from DHS.

10.2   Jurisdiction

Where a DHS officer enters an adverse decision against an individual or carrier in a fines case, an appeal may be taken to the Board. 8 C.F.R. § 1280.1(b).

10.3   Processing

(a) Standing — Only the individual or carrier being fined may file an appeal. However, if that individual or carrier admits the allegations in the Notice of Intent to Fine or does not answer it, the opportunity to appeal is waived. See 8 C.F.R. § 1280.1.

(b) Filing the Appeal —

(1) How to file — Fine appeals are made on the Notice of Appeal (Form EOIR-29). 8 C.F.R. § 1003.3(a)(2). (This form is different from the Form EOIR-26 used in immigration court proceedings.)

(2) Where to file — Unlike appeals from the decisions of immigration judges, fine appeals are filed with DHS, in accordance with the applicable regulations and any instructions that appear on the DHS decision. See generally 8 C.F.R. § 1003.3(a)(2). The appeal must be filed with the DHS office having administrative control over the fine record.

(3) When to file — A fine appeal must be filed within 15 days after the mailing of the notification of decision. See 8 C.F.R. § 1280.1.

(4) Fee — The filing fee for a fine appeal is $110. See 8 C.F.R. § 1003.8(b). Unlike appeals of immigration judge decisions, the fee is filed directly with DHS, in accordance with DHS instructions. The fee should be paid in the manner instructed by DHS.

(5) Representation — An individual or carrier appealing a fine decision may be represented by a practitioner of record through the filing of a Notice of Appearance (Form EOIR-27). See generally Chapter 2.1(b) (Entering an Appearance as the Practitioner of Record). The practitioner should file the Form EOIR-27 directly with DHS, together with the Notice of Appeal (Form EOIR-29. See 8 C.F.R. § 1292.4(a). Until the Board confirms that it has received the fine record from DHS, as discussed in subsection (c) below, practitioners must submit the Form EOIR-27 directly with DHS and should not submit a Form EOIR-27 directly with the Board. Any Form EOIR-27 received prior to the Board receiving the fine record will not be recognized and will not be forwarded to DHS for inclusion in the fine record. Note that the Form EOIR-27 is not the one used to appear before DHS (Notice of Entry of Appearance as Attorney or Accredited Representative (Form G-28)) and that the Board will not recognize a practitioner using Form G-28.

Practitioners are not permitted to make a limited appearance for document assistance through the Notice of Limited Appearance (Form EOIR-60) in cases involving appeals of fine decisions adjudicated before the Board. Any Form EOIR-60 and the associated assisted documents will not be recognized and will be rejected. Practitioners that provide document assistance in such cases must file a Notice of Appearance (Form EOIR-27) as discussed above. See Chapter 2.1(c)(3) (Limited Appearances for Document Assistance Only Permitted in Cases that Originated in the Immigration Court).

(6) Supporting briefs — Briefs, if desired, are filed with DHS, at the same office as the Notice of Appeal (Form EOIR-29) and in accordance with any briefing schedule set by DHS. See 8 C.F.R. § 1003.3(c)(2). Requests to extend the time for filing a brief should be directed to DHS. The Board may, in its discretion, authorize briefs to be filed directly with the Board. 8 C.F.R. § 1003.3(c)(2).

Absent special instructions from DHS, briefs on fine appeals should generally follow the guidelines set forth in Chapters 3.3 (Documents) and 4.6 (Appeal Briefs).

(7) Evidence — The Board does not consider new evidence on appeal. If new evidence is submitted in the course of an appeal, the submission may be deemed a motion to remand the matter to DHS for consideration of that new evidence. If the individual or carrier wishes to submit new evidence, that individual or carrier should articulate the purpose of the new evidence and explain its prior unavailability. Any document submitted to the Board should comport with the guidelines set forth in Chapter 3.3 (Documents).

However, the Board will not consider evidence or remand the matter where the proffered evidence was expressly requested by DHS and a reasonable opportunity to provide it was given before the matter was adjudicated by DHS. *Matter of Soriano*, 19 I&N Dec. 764 (BIA 1988).

(8) Stipulations — The Board encourages the parties, whenever possible, to stipulate to any facts or events that pertain to the adjudication of the appeal.

(9) Electronic filing — Fine cases are not available for electronic filing through ECAS. Accordingly, all documents related to fine proceeding before the Board must be submitted as a paper filings.

(c) Processing — Once an appeal has been properly filed with DHS and the record is complete, DHS forwards the record to the Board for adjudication of the appeal. After the Board receives the record from DHS, the Board issues a notice to the parties acknowledging receipt of the record and appeal.

(1) Record on appeal — The record on appeal consists of all decisions and documents in the record, including some or all of the following items: the Notice of Intent to Fine, any written defense or correspondence, any documentary evidence submitted to DHS, the record of any personal interviews, the DHS decision, the Notice of Appeal, any briefs on appeal, the record of any prior DHS action, and the record of any prior Board action.

(2) Briefing schedule — Briefing schedules are issued by DHS and are to be completed prior to the forwarding of the record to the Board. Accordingly, the Board generally does not issue briefing schedules in fine cases.

(3) Status inquiries/DHS — Until the record is received by the Board, all status inquiries must be directed to the DHS office where the appeal was filed. *The Board has no record of the appeal until the record is received by the Board.* Since the Board and DHS are distinct and separate entities, the Board cannot track or provide information on cases that remain within the possession of DHS.

(4) Status inquiries/Board — Confirmation that the Board has received a fine record from DHS can be obtained from the Clerk's Office. See Appendix A (Directory). The Board tracks fine appeals by the name and an assigned case number for the individual or carrier. All status inquiries should contain this information. See generally Chapter 1.6(a) (All Communications).

(5) Adjudication — Upon the entry of a decision, the Board serves the decision upon the parties by regular mail. An order issued by the Board is final, unless and until it is stayed, modified, rescinded, or overruled by the Board, the Attorney General, or a federal court. An order is deemed effective as of its issuance date unless the order provides otherwise. See Chapter 1.4(d) (Board Decisions).

(d) Motions — Motions filed during the pendency of an appeal should be filed where the fine record is located. Motions may not be filed with the Board until the record has been received by the Board. See Chapter 10.3(c)(4) (Status inquiries/Board).

All motions filed subsequent to the Board's adjudication of an appeal, including motions to reopen and motions to reconsider the Board's decision, are to be filed with the DHS office having administrative control over the record, not with the Board. 8 C.F.R. § 1003.2(g)(2)(ii).

(e) Withdrawal of Appeal — The appeal may, at any time prior to the entry of a decision by the Board, be voluntarily withdrawn. To withdraw an appeal, the individual or carrier should file a written request, with a cover page labeled "WITHDRAWAL OF FINE APPEAL," with either DHS or the Board, whichever holds the file at the time the withdrawal is submitted. See Chapter 4.11 (Withdrawing an Appeal), Appendix E

(Cover Pages). If the appeal is before the Board, Proof of Service on DHS should be submitted with the withdrawal. See Chapters 3.2(d) (Proof of Service), 4.11 (Withdrawing an Appeal).

10.4 Personal Interviews

(a) Remand — The Board has the authority to request or direct a personal interview of the individual or carrier. See 8 C.F.R. § 1280.1. A remand may be warranted when DHS enters a decision without granting a personal interview, either initially or on remand. See 8 C.F.R. § 1280.1. A remand may also be warranted when the DHS decision does not adequately state the reasons for assessing the fine. *Matter of Air India "Flight No. 101"*, 21 I&N Dec. 890 (BIA 1997).

(b) Invalidation of Fine — If DHS fails to grant an interview, the Board may invalidate the fine. *Matter of "Beechcraft B-95, #N21JC"*, 17 I&N Dec. 147 (BIA 1979).

Chapter 11 Discipline

11.1   Practitioner and Recognized Organization Discipline Generally

The Board has the authority to impose disciplinary sanctions upon practitioners and recognized organizations who violate rules of professional conduct in practice before the Board, the immigration courts, and the Department of Homeland Security (DHS). 8 C.F.R. §§ 1003.1(b)(13), (d)(2)(iii), (d)(5); 1003.101-111; 292.3; 1292.3. See also *Matter of Gadda*, 23 I&N Dec. 645 (BIA 2003).

11.2   Definition of Practitioner and Recognized Organizations

The term "practitioner" refers to an individual's or entity's attorney or representative, as defined in 8 C.F.R. §§ 1001.1(f), 1001.1(j), 1001.1(ff), and 1292.1(a)-(b) respectively. The term "representative" refers to non-attorneys authorized to practice before the immigration courts and the Board of Immigration Appeals, including law students and law graduates, reputable individuals, accredited representatives, accredited officials, and persons formerly authorized to practice. See 8 C.F.R. §§ 1001.1(j), 1292.1(a)-(b).

The term "recognized organization" is defined as a non-profit, federal tax-exempt, religious, charitable, social service, or similar organization established in the United States that has been recognized by the Assistant Director for Policy or the Assistant Director's designee to represent noncitizens through accredited representatives before DHS only or before the Board, the immigration courts, and DHS. See 8 C.F.R. § 1292.11.

11.3   Jurisdiction

(a) **Practitioners** — The Board is authorized to discipline any practitioner if the Board finds it to be in the public interest to do so. 8 C.F.R. §§ 1003.101(a), 292.3(a). Pursuant to regulations, it is in the public interest to discipline any practitioner who has engaged in criminal, unethical, or unprofessional conduct or in frivolous behavior. 8 C.F.R. §§ 1003.101(a), 1003.102, 292.3(b).

(b) **Recognized Organizations** — The Board is authorized to discipline a recognized organization if the Board finds it to be in the public interest to do so. 8 C.F.R. §§ 1003.110, 1003.111. It is in the public interest to discipline a recognized organization that violates one or more of the grounds specified in 8 C.F.R. §§ 1003.110(b), 1292.3.

(c) **DHS Attorneys** — The Board's disciplinary authority does not extend to attorneys who represent DHS. The conduct of DHS attorneys is governed by DHS rules and regulations. Concerns or complaints about the conduct of DHS attorneys should be raised with DHS.

(d) **Immigration Judges** — The Board's disciplinary authority does not extend to immigration judges. When a party has an immediate concern regarding an immigration judge's conduct that is not appropriate for a motion or appeal, the concern may be raised with the Assistant Chief Immigration Judge (ACIJ) responsible for the court or the

ACIJ for Conduct and Professionalism. Contact information for ACIJs is available on EOIR's website.

In the alternative, parties may raise concerns regarding an immigration judge's conduct directly with the Office of the Director by following the procedures outlined on the EOIR website.

(e) Immigration Specialists/Consultants — The Board does not have authority to discipline individuals such as "immigration specialists," "visa consultants," "notarios," and other individuals who engage in the unauthorized practice of law. However, the Board has the authority to discipline practitioners who assist in the unauthorized practice of law. 8 C.F.R. § 1003.102(m). The Board encourages anyone harmed by the unauthorized practice of law to report it to the appropriate law enforcement, consumer protection, and other authorities. In addition, persons harmed by such conduct are encouraged to contact the Executive Office for Immigration Review Fraud Program. See Chapter 1.2(f)(2) (Office of the General Counsel), Appendix A (Directory).

11.4 Conduct

(a) Practitioners — A practitioner may be disciplined by the Board for:

- frivolous behavior, as defined in 8 C.F.R. § 1003.102(j) and discussed at 8 C.F.R. § 1003.1(d)(2)(iii)

- ineffective assistance of counsel as provided in 8 C.F.R. § 1003.102(k)

- misconduct resulting in disbarment from, suspension by, or resignation from a state or federal licensing authority while a disciplinary investigation or proceeding is pending

- conviction of a serious crime

- a false statement of material fact or law made knowingly or with reckless disregard

- false certification of a copy of a document made knowingly or with reckless disregard

- assisting the unauthorized practice of law

- grossly excessive fees

- bribery, coercion, or an attempt at either, with the intention of affecting the outcome of an immigration case

- improper solicitation of clients or using "runners"

- misrepresenting qualifications or services

- repeated failure to appear for scheduled hearings in a timely manner without good cause

- courtroom conduct that would constitute contempt of court in a judicial proceeding

- engaging in conduct prejudicial to administration of justice

- failing to provide competent representation

- failing to abide by a client's decision

- failing to act with reasonable diligence

- failing to maintain communication with a client

- failing to disclose legal authority to an adjudicator

- repeatedly failing to submit a signed and completed appearance form in compliance with the applicable rules and regulations

- repeatedly drafting notices, motions, briefs, or claims, which are filed with DHS or EOIR, that reflect little or no attention to the specific factual or legal issues applicable to a client's case, but rather rely on boilerplate language indicative of a substantive failure to completely and diligently represent the client

- repeatedly failing to sign any pleading, application, motion, petition, brief, or other document that the practitioner prepared or drafted and was filed with EOIR

See 8 C.F.R. § 1003.102. This list is not exhaustive or exclusive, and other grounds for discipline may be identified by the Board. 8 C.F.R. § 1003.102.

(b) Recognized Organizations — A recognized organization may be disciplined by the Board for:

- Making false statements or providing misleading information in applying for recognition or accreditation of its representative

- misrepresenting scope of authority or services

- failing to provide adequate supervision of accredited representatives

- engaging in the practice of law through staff when organization does not have an attorney or accredited representative

See 8 C.F.R. § 1003.110. This list is not exhaustive or exclusive, and other grounds for discipline may be identified by the Board. 8 C.F.R. § 1003.110.

11.5 Complaints

(a) Who May File — Anyone may file a complaint against a practitioner or recognized organization, including aggrieved clients, adjudicators, DHS personnel, and other practitioners. 8 C.F.R. §§ 1003.104(a)(1), 1292.19(a).

(b) What to File — Complaints must be submitted in writing. Persons filing complaints are encouraged to use the Immigration Practitioner/Organization Complaint Form (Form EOIR 44), which can be downloaded from the EOIR website. See Chapter 12.2(b) (Obtaining Forms), Appendix D (Forms). The complaint form provides important information about the complaint process, confidentiality, and the kinds of misconduct that the Board can discipline. Complaints should be specific and as detailed as possible, providing supporting documentation when it is available.

(c) Where to File —

(1) Misconduct before Board or immigration judge — Complaints alleging misconduct before the Board or an immigration court are filed with the Office of the General Counsel of the Executive Office for Immigration Review (EOIR). 8 C.F.R. § 1003.104(a)(1). The completed form and supporting documents should be sent to:

Office of the General Counsel
Executive Office for Immigration Review
5107 Leesburg Pike, Suite 2600
Falls Church, VA 22041
Attn: Disciplinary Counsel

OR

EOIR.Attorney.Discipline@usdoj.gov

After receiving the complaint, the EOIR Disciplinary Counsel decides whether or not to initiate disciplinary proceedings. 8 C.F.R. § 1003.104(b).

(2) Misconduct before DHS — Complaints involving such conduct before DHS are to be filed with the DHS Disciplinary Counsel. 8 C.F.R. §§ 1003.104(a)(2); 292.3(d).

(d) When to File — Complaints should be filed as soon as possible. There are no time limits for filing most complaints. However, complaints based on ineffective assistance of counsel must be filed within one year of a finding of ineffective assistance of counsel by the Board, the immigration court, or a federal court judge or panel. 8 C.F.R. § 1003.102(k).

11.6 Duty to Report

A practitioner who practices before the Board, the immigration courts, or DHS and, if applicable, the authorized officer of each recognized organization with which a practitioner is affiliated, has an affirmative duty to report whenever the practitioner:

- has been found guilty of, or pled guilty or nolo contendere to, a serious crime (as defined in 8 C.F.R. § 1003.102(h)), or

- has been suspended or disbarred, or has resigned with an admission of misconduct, or has resigned while a disciplinary investigation or proceeding is pending

8 C.F.R. § 1003.103(c). The practitioner and, if applicable, the authorized official of each recognized organization must report the misconduct, criminal conviction, or discipline to the EOIR Disciplinary Counsel within 30 days of the issuance of the relevant initial order. The practitioner also must report the misconduct, criminal

conviction, or discipline to the DHS Disciplinary Counsel within 30 days of issuance of the relevant initial order. 8 C.F.R. § 292.3(c)(4). The duty to report applies even if an appeal of the conviction or discipline is pending. The EOIR Disciplinary Counsel may be reached at the mailing and email address listed above.

11.7 Procedure

The regulations provide the procedures for filing complaints and imposing sanctions for misconduct before the Board and the immigration courts. See 8 C.F.R. § 1003.101 et seq. The regulations also contain procedures for filing complaints regarding misconduct before DHS. 8 C.F.R. §§ 292.3; 1292.3.

(a) Initiation of Proceedings —

(1) Notice of Intent to Discipline — Disciplinary proceedings begin when the EOIR Disciplinary Counsel or the DHS Disciplinary Counsel files a Notice of Intent to Discipline with the Board and serves a copy on the practitioner and/or authorized officer of the organization. The Notice contains a statement of the charge(s) against the practitioner and/or recognized organization, a copy of the inquiry report (if any), proposed disciplinary sanctions, the procedure for filing an answer to the Notice or requesting a hearing, and the contact information for the Board. 8 C.F.R. §§ 1003.105(a), 292.3.

(2) Petition for Immediate Suspension — When the Notice of Intent to Discipline concerns a practitioner who has either been convicted of a serious crime or is subject to suspension or disbarment by a state or federal licensing authority, the EOIR Disciplinary Counsel or the DHS Disciplinary Counsel may petition for the immediate suspension of that attorney. 8 C.F.R. §§ 1003.103(a)(1), 1292.3, 292.3(c).

Usually filed in conjunction with the Notice of Intent to Discipline, the petition for immediate suspension seeks the practitioner's immediate suspension from practice before the Board and the immigration courts. 8 C.F.R. § 1003.103(a). DHS may ask that the practitioner be similarly suspended from practice before DHS.

The regulations direct that, upon the filing of a petition for immediate suspension, the Board will suspend the practitioner for as long as disciplinary proceedings are pending. 8 C.F.R. § 1003.103(a)(4). The regulations permit the immediate suspension to be set aside when the Board deems it in the interest of justice to do so. 8 C.F.R. § 1003.103(a)(4). The usual hardships that accompany a suspension from practice (e.g., loss of income, duty to complete pending cases) are generally not sufficient to set aside an immediate suspension order. *Matter of Rosenberg*, 24 I&N Dec. 744, 745 (BIA 2009).

(3) Petition for Interim Suspension — In conjunction with the Notice of Intent to Discipline or at any time during the disciplinary proceedings, the EOIR Disciplinary Counsel may petition for an interim suspension from practice of an accredited representative before the Board and the immigration courts. 8 C.F.R.

§ 1003.111(a)(1). DHS may ask that the accredited representative be similarly suspended from practice before DHS. 8 C.F.R. § 1003.111(a)(2).

In the petition, counsel for the government must demonstrate by a preponderance of the evidence that the accredited representative poses a substantial threat of irreparable harm. 8 C.F.R. § 1003.111(a)(3).

(b) Response — The subject of a Notice of Intent to Discipline has 30 days from the date of service to file a written answer to the Notice and to request a hearing. 8 C.F.R. § 1003.105(c)(1). An answer is deemed filed at the time it is received by the Board. See Chapter 3.1(b) (Must be "Timely"). The answer should be served on both the EOIR Disciplinary Counsel and the DHS Disciplinary Counsel. The time in which to file an answer may be extended for good cause shown through the filing of a motion no later than 3 working days before the filing deadline. 8 C.F.R. § 1003.105(c)(1).

In the answer, the practitioner who is subject to summary disciplinary proceedings must make a prima facie showing to the Board that there is a material issue of fact in dispute with regard to the basis for the proceedings, or that one of the exceptions set forth in the regulations applies. 8 C.F.R. § 1003.106(a)(1).

(1) Timely answer — If the answer to summary disciplinary proceedings is timely and the Board determines that there is a material issue of fact in dispute or that one of the exceptions set forth in the regulations applies, the matter will be referred to the Chief Immigration Judge for appointment of an appropriate adjudicator, generally an immigration judge, to conduct a disciplinary hearing. 8 C.F.R. § 1003.106(a)(1). The answer of a practitioner or, in cases involving recognized organizations, the organization, must specifically admit or deny each of the allegations in the Notice of Intent to Discipline. Each allegation not denied is deemed admitted. 8 C.F.R. § 1003.105(c)(2).

If the practitioner or, in cases involving recognized organizations, the organization, wishes to have a hearing, the request for a hearing must be contained in the written answer. Otherwise, the opportunity to request a hearing will be deemed waived. 8 C.F.R. § 1003.105(c)(3).

Regardless of whether a hearing has been requested, the Board will refer a case to the Chief Immigration Judge for appointment of an adjudicator if the case involves a charge or charges that cannot be adjudicated under the summary disciplinary proceeding provisions. 8 C.F.R. § 1003.106(a)(1). If the practitioner fails to make a prima facie showing that there is a material issue of fact in dispute or that one of the exceptions set forth in the regulations applies, the Board shall issue a final order imposing discipline.

(2) No answer or untimely answer — If the Board does not receive a timely answer, the failure to answer is deemed an admission of the allegations in the Notice of Intent to Discipline, and the practitioner is thereafter precluded from requesting a hearing on the matter. 8 C.F.R. § 1003.105(d). The regulations require the Board to enter a default order imposing the discipline recommended by the EOIR Disciplinary Counsel and the DHS Disciplinary Counsel, absent the presence of special considerations. 8 C.F.R. § 1003.105(d)(2).

A practitioner or the organization subject to a default order may move to set aside that order, provided that the motion is filed within 15 days of the date of service of the default order and that the practitioner's or organization's failure to answer was due to exceptional circumstances beyond the control of the practitioner or recognized organization (e.g., the practitioner serious illness, death of an immediate relative). 8 C.F.R. § 1003.105(d)(2).

(c) Hearing — If the matter is referred to the Chief Immigration Judge, the disciplinary hearings will largely be conducted in the same manner as immigration proceedings. 8 C.F.R. § 1003.106. However, the immigration judge presiding over the disciplinary proceeding will not be one before whom the practitioner regularly appears. 8 C.F.R. § 1003.106(a)(1)(i).

(d) Appeals — The regulations provide that the Board may entertain an appeal filed by a practitioner or, in cases involving a recognized organization, the organization, wishing to challenge the adjudicator's disciplinary ruling. 8 C.F.R. § 1003.106(c). The appeal must be received by the Board within 30 days of the oral decision or, if no oral decision was rendered, 30 days of the date of mailing of the written decision. The proper form for filing a practitioner/organization discipline appeal is the Notice of Appeal (Form EOIR-45), which can be downloaded from the EOIR website. See Chapter 12.2(b) (Obtaining Forms), Appendix D (Forms). This form is specific to disciplinary proceedings and is different from the Notices of Appeal in other types of proceedings. See Appendix D (Forms). The parties must comply with all of the other standard provisions (non ECAS-related) for filing appeals with the Board. 8 C.F.R. § 1003.106(c). See Chapter 4 (Appeals of Immigration Judge Decisions). These appeals may not be submitted electronically.

(e) Motions — As with most motions in immigration proceedings, motions should be filed with the adjudicator who has jurisdiction over the case.

11.8 Sanctions

The Board is authorized to impose a broad range of sanctions against practitioners, including "disbarment" (permanent suspension) from immigration practice, public or private censure, and other sanctions deemed appropriate by the Board. 8 C.F.R. § 1003.101(a). The Board may even increase the level of disciplinary sanction. *Matter of Gadda*, 23 I&N Dec. 645 (BIA 2003). The Board is also authorized to impose sanctions against a recognized organization, including revocation, termination, and such other sanctions as deemed appropriate. 8 C.F.R. § 1003.110.

When a practitioner has been disbarred or suspended, that information is made available to the public on the EOIR website, at the Board, and at the immigration courts. See Chapter 11.9 (Confidentiality).

11.9   Confidentiality

The regulations discuss confidentiality and public disclosure at the various stages of disciplinary proceedings. See 8 C.F.R. § 1003.108. As a general rule, action taken on a Notice of Intent to Discipline may be disclosed to the public. 8 C.F.R. § 1003.108(c).

11.10 Effect on Cases Before the Board

(a) Duty to Advise Clients — A practitioner or organization who is disciplined is obligated to advise all clients with a case pending before either the Board or an immigration court that they been disciplined by the Board.

(b) Pending Cases Deemed Unrepresented — Once a practitioner has been disciplined by the Board and is currently not authorized to practice before the Board and the immigration courts, the Board will deem that practitioner's pending cases to be unrepresented. Filings that are submitted after a practitioner has been disbarred or suspended will be rejected and returned to the party whenever possible. If the practitioner is later reinstated by the Board, the practitioner must file a new Notice of Entry of Appearance (Form EOIR-27) in every case, even if the practitioner previously represented that party. See Chapter 11.12(d) (Cases Pending at the Time of Reinstatement).

(c) Ineffective Assistance of Counsel — The imposition of discipline on a practitioner does not constitute per se evidence of ineffective assistance of counsel in any case formerly represented by that practitioner.

(d) Filing Deadlines — An order of practitioner or organization discipline does not automatically excuse parties from meeting any applicable filing deadlines.

11.11 List of Suspended and Expelled Attorneys

A list of practitioners who have been suspended or disbarred from immigration practice appears on EOIR's website. The list is updated periodically. Copies are also posted at the Board and in the immigration courts.

11.12 Reinstatement

(a) Expiration of Suspension — When a period of suspension has run, reinstatement is not automatic. 8 C.F.R. § 1003.107(a). With exceptions for accredited representatives specified in subsection (c), a practitioner who has been suspended from immigration practice and who wishes to be reinstated must:

- file a motion with the Board requesting to be reinstated

- show that they can meet the definition of "attorney" set forth in 8 C.F.R. § 1001.1(f) (or § 1001.1(j) if a "representative")

- serve a copy of such motion on the EOIR Disciplinary Counsel and the DHS Disciplinary Counsel. 8 C.F.R. § 1003.107(a)(1)

The EOIR Disciplinary Counsel or the DHS Disciplinary Counsel may file a written response, including supporting documents or evidence, objecting to reinstatement on the ground that the practitioner failed to comply with the terms of the suspension. 8 C.F.R. § 1003.107(a)(2). Failure to meet the definition of an attorney or representative will result in the request for reinstatement being denied. 8 C.F.R. § 1003.107(b)(3). If the practitioner failed to comply with the terms of the suspension, the Board will deny the motion and indicate the circumstances under which reinstatement may be sought.

(b) Petition for Early Reinstatement — With exceptions for accredited representatives specified in subsection (c), a practitioner who has been disbarred or has been suspended for a year or more may seek early reinstatement with the Board if the practitioner:

- petitions after one year or one-half of the term of suspension has expired, whichever is greater

- can meet the regulatory definition of "attorney" or "representative," as applicable, in 8 C.F.R. § 1001.1(f) or § 1001.1(j)

- can demonstrate by clear, unequivocal, and convincing evidence that the practitioner possesses the moral and professional qualifications required to return to immigration practice

- can show that reinstatement will not be detrimental to the administration of justice

8 C.F.R. § 1003.107(b)(1). *Matter of Krivonos*, 24 I&N Dec. 292, 293 (BIA 2007). Failure to meet any one of these criteria will result in the request for reinstatement being denied. Once a request for reinstatement is denied, the practitioner may not seek reinstatement for another full year unless the practitioner is eligible under subsection (a) above. 8 C.F.R. § 1003.107(b)(3). The Board may, in its discretion, hold a hearing to determine if the practitioner meets all the regulatory requirements for reinstatement.

Requests for reinstatement must be served on the EOIR Disciplinary Counsel and the DHS Disciplinary Counsel. 8 C.F.R. § 1003.107(b)(1).

(c) Accredited Representatives —

(1) Suspended — When an accredited representative is suspended past the expiration of the period of accreditation, the representative may not seek reinstatement. After the representative's suspension period has expired, a new request for accreditation may be submitted by the recognized organization pursuant to 8 C.F.R. § 1292.13. 8 C.F.R. § 1003.107(c)(1).

(2) Disbarred — An accredited representative who has been disbarred may not seek reinstatement. 8 C.F.R. § 1003.107(c)(2).

(d) Cases Pending at the Time of Reinstatement — Suspension or disbarment by the Board terminates representation. A practitioner reinstated to immigration practice by the Board who wishes to represent individuals before the Board or the immigration courts must enter a new appearance in each case, even if the practitioner was the practitioner of record at the time that discipline was imposed. The practitioner should include proof of reinstatement with each new appearance. See Chapter 2.1 (Representation and Appearances Generally).

Chapter 12 Forms

12.1 Forms Generally

There is an official form that must be used to:

- file an appeal - see Chapter 4.4(b) (Notice of Appeal)

- request a fee waiver - see Chapter 3.4 (Filing Fees)

- appear as a practitioner of record - see Chapter 2.1(b) (Entering an Appearance as Practitioner of Record)

- disclose document assistance through limited appearance - see Chapter 2.1(c) (Limited Appearance for Document Assistance)

- report a change of address - see Chapter 2.2(c) (Address Obligations)

- request most kinds of relief - see 8 C.F.R. parts 299, 1299

There is an official form that should be used to:

- file a practitioner or recognized organization complaint - see Chapter 11.5 (Complaints)

There is no official form to:

- file a motion - see Chapter 5.2(b) (Form)

An appeal form, such as the Form EOIR-26, should *never* be used to file a motion.

12.2 Obtaining Blank Forms

(a) Identifying EOIR Forms — Many forms used by the Executive Office for Immigration Review (EOIR) do not appear in the regulations. Form names and numbers can be obtained from the clerks of most immigration courts and the Clerk's Office of the Board. See Appendix A (Directory). All of the forms most commonly used by the public are identified in this manual. See Appendix D (Forms).

(b) Obtaining Forms — Appendix D (Forms) contains a list of frequently requested forms and information on where to obtain them. In general, EOIR forms are available from the following sources:

- the EOIR website

- the local immigration court

- the Clerk's Office, Board of Immigration Appeals

- certain Government Printing Office (GPO) Bookstores

Parties should be sure to use the most recent version of each form, which will be available from the sources listed here.

(c) Photocopied Forms — Photocopies of blank EOIR forms may be used, provided that they are an accurate duplication of the government issued form and are printed on the correct size and stock of paper. See 8 C.F.R. §§ 299.4(a), 1299.1. The filing party is responsible for the accuracy and legibility of the form. If colored paper is used, it should comply with subsection (e) below. The paper used to photocopy the form should also comply with Chapter 3.3(c)(4) (Paper size and quality). The most recent version of the form must be used and is available from the sources listed in subsection (b), above.

(d) Computer-Generated Forms — Computer-generated versions of EOIR forms may be used, provided that they are an accurate duplication of the government-issued form and are printed on the correct size and stock of paper. See 8 C.F.R. §§ 299.4(a), 1299.1. The filing party is responsible for the accuracy and legibility of the form. If colored paper is used, it should comply with subsection (e) below. The paper used to photocopy the form should also comply with Chapter 3.3(c)(4) (Paper size and quality). The most recent version of the form must be used and is available from the sources listed in subsection (b), above. The electronic submission of the Form EOIR-27 may only be made, at this time, by registered attorneys and fully accredited representatives. See Chapter 2.1(b) (Entering an Appearance as Practitioner of Record); 3.1(a)(6) (Electronic filing through ECAS) .

(e) Form Colors — The Board no longer requires forms to be filed on paper of a specific color. All forms may now be filed on white paper. Any submission that is not a form must be on white paper.

The use of colored paper is still welcome, but only in the following instances:

- Blue - EOIR-26 (Notice of Appeal/Immigration Judge Decision)

- Tan - EOIR-26A (Fee Waiver Request)

- Yellow - EOIR-27 (Notice of Appearance)

- Pink - EOIR-29 (Notice of Appeal/DHS decision)

- Pink - EOIR-33/BIA (Change of Address)

(f) Non-Form Filings — Where a filing is not form-based (e.g., a motion or a request), the Board strongly recommends the use of a cover page. See Appendix E (Cover Pages).

12.3 Submitting Completed Forms

The Board will accept photocopies of completed forms, provided that the original completed form bears an original signature and is available to the Board upon request. The most recent version of the form must be used and is available from the sources listed in Chapter 12.2(b) (Obtaining Forms). All filing requirements should be observed. See Chapter 3 (Filings with the Board). See also Chapters 4 (Appeals of Immigration Judge Decisions), 5 (Motions before the Board), 7 (Bond), 9 (Visa Petitions), 10 (Fines).

Chapter 13 Requesting Records

13.1 Generally

The Freedom of Information Act (FOIA) provides the public access, with certain exceptions, to federal agency records. See 5 U.S.C. § 552. The Office of the General Counsel, Executive Office for Immigration Review, FOIA Service Center responds to FOIA requests for Board records.

13.2 Requests

(a) Who May File —

(1) Parties —

(A) Inspecting the record — Parties to a proceeding, and their practitioners of record, may inspect the official record of proceedings. A FOIA request is not required. Inspection by prior arrangement with the Board Clerk's Office is strongly recommended to ensure that the official record of proceedings is immediately available. See Chapter 1.5(e) (Records). Parties to a proceeding before the Board may request inspection by calling the Clerk's Office. See Appendix A (Directory). Parties may review all portions of the record that are not prohibited (e.g., classified information, documents under a protective order). EOIR prohibits the removal of official records by parties or other persons from EOIR-controlled space.

(B) Obtaining copies of record — The Board does not automatically provide a copy of the official record of proceedings to the parties to the proceedings upon the filing of an appeal or motion. The Clerk's Office will provide copies of the official record of proceedings to parties and their practitioners of record upon request. A FOIA request is not required. Parties may obtain a copy of all portions of the record that are not prohibited (e.g., classified information, documents under a protective order). See Chapter 1.5(e) (Records). To request a copy from the BIA, email "EOIR.BIA.ROP.Requests@usdoj.gov". This email address is only to be used for requests for a copy of the official record. The Board does not provide self-service copying.

(2) Non-parties — Persons who are not party to a proceeding before the Board must file a request with the Office of the General Counsel, Executive Office for Immigration Review, if they wish to see or obtain copies of the record of proceedings.

(b) How to File —

(1) Form — FOIA requests must be made in writing. See 28 C.F.R. § 16.1 et seq. Although the Executive Office for Immigration Review (EOIR) does not have an official form for filing FOIA requests, the Form EOIR-59, Certification and Release of Records, can be used in conjunction with a FOIA request when requesting third party information. See Appendix D (Forms). The Department of Homeland Security Freedom of Information/Privacy Act Request (Form G-639) should not be used to file such requests. Requests may be submitted through the Public Access Link available on EOIR's website or may be mailed to:

> U.S. Department of Justice
> Executive Office for Immigration Review
> Office of the General Counsel – FOIA Service Center
> FOIA/Privacy Act Requests
> 5107 Leesburg Pike, Suite 2150
> Falls Church, VA 22041

For more information, contact the EOIR FOIA Service Center. See Appendix A (Directory).

    (2) Information required — Requests should thoroughly describe the records sought and include as much identifying information as possible regarding names, dates, subject matter, and location of proceedings. For example, if a request pertains to a respondent in removal proceedings, the request should contain the full name and A-number of that respondent. The more precise and comprehensive the information provided in the FOIA request, the better and more expeditiously the request can be processed.

    (3) Fee — There is no fee to file a FOIA request, but fees may be charged for the review, search, and reproduction of records. See 28 C.F.R. § 16.3(c).

    (4) Processing times — Processing times for FOIA requests vary, depending on such factors as the nature of the request and the location of the record.

(c) When to File —

    (1) Time — A FOIA request should be filed as soon as possible, especially when a party is facing a filing deadline. Parties should not wait to receive a briefing schedule or other response from the Board before submitting a FOIA request.

    (2) Effect on filing deadlines — Parties should not delay the filing of an appeal, motion, brief, or other document while awaiting a response to a FOIA request. Failure to receive FOIA materials prior to a filing deadline does not excuse the party from meeting a filing deadline.

(d) Limitations —

    (1) Statutory exemptions — Certain information in agency records, such as classified material and information that would cause a clearly unwarranted invasion of personal privacy, is exempted from release under the Freedom of Information Act. 5 U.S.C. § 552(b)(1)-(9). Where appropriate, records of redacted (*e.g.*, removed or cut out) and copies of the redacted material are provided to the requested person. When material is redacted, the reason or reasons for the redaction are indicated.

(2) Agency's duty — The FOIA statute does not require the Executive Office for Immigration Review, its Office of the General Counsel, or the Board to perform legal research, nor does it entitle the requesting person to copies of documents that are available for sale or on the internet.

(3) Subject's consent — When a FOIA request seeks information that is exempt from disclosure on the grounds of personal privacy, the subject of the record (*e.g.*, the respondent, the petitioner, the carrier) must consent in writing to the release of that information.

13.3 Denials

If a FOIA request is denied, in whole or in part, the requesting party may appeal that decision to the Office of Information and Privacy, Department of Justice. Information on how to appeal the denial of a FOIA request is available on the Office of Information and Privacy's website. The rules regarding FOIA appeals can be found at 28 C.F.R. § 16.9.

This page intentionally left blank.

Chapter 14 Other Information

14.1 Reproduction of the Board Practice Manual

This Practice Manual is a public document that may be reproduced without advance authorization from the Board.

14.2 Updates to the Board Practice Manual

The current version of this Practice Manual, which includes all updates, is posted on EOIR's website. Parties should make sure to consult the most recent version of the Practice Manual.

14.3 Public Input

(a) Practice Manual — The Board welcomes and encourages the public to provide comments on this Practice Manual, to identify errors or ambiguities in this text, and to propose revisions to improve this text in the future.

Correspondence should be addressed to the Chief Appellate Immigration Judge of the Board of Immigration Appeals. See Appendix A (Directory). The public is asked not to combine comments on this Practice Manual with inquiries regarding specific cases pending before the Board.

(b) Regulations and Published Rules — Periodically, the Executive Office for Immigration Review engages in federal rulemaking in the Federal Register. Immigration regulations are revised to better effectuate existing law and to comport with new law as it is promulgated. The public is encouraged to participate in the rulemaking process.

New regulations are published in the Federal Register, which is available online at www.ofr.gov, in most law libraries, and in many public libraries. Copies of the Federal Register are also available from the Government Printing Office (GPO) for purchase. Call (202) 512-1800 (not a toll-free call) or (866) 512-1800 (toll free) or visit the GPO website at www.gpo.gov for more information on GPO publications and bookstore locations.

This page intentionally left blank.

Index

Citation Index

A separate Word Index precedes this index.